Piggy The Cat and Arcade Matt

KAREN MALENA

Copyright

Piggy the Cat and Arcade Matt

Karen Malena

Copyright © 2023 Karen Malena
All rights reserved. No part of this book may be reproduced in any form or by any electronic or mechanical means, including information storage and retrieval systems, without the express written consent of the publisher, except by a reviewer, who may quote brief passages in a review.

AIW Press, LLC
Lower Burrell, Pennsylvania
aiwpress.com

ISBN: 978-1-944938-38

Contents

Foreword	vii
Piggy Finds a Home	1
One	3
Piggy's Ode to Food	15
Piggy Poetry	17
Photos of Me	35
Piggy's Big Adventure	51
Prologue	53
Chapter 1	55
Chapter 2	69
Chapter 3	81
Chapter 4	103
About the Author	121

Dedication

For Ella, Lyla, McKenna & Amelia

May your imaginations soar.

Foreword

In 2013, I published a book simply called "Piggy" with a fun, adventurous story of cat, mouse, and other silly characters. It has since gone out of publication but I wanted to put together a compilation of some poetry I penned on Piggy the cat's Facebook page, a heartfelt, true rendition of how Arcade Matt became Piggy's beloved human, and also the original older fiction story with a new, fun twist and title.

Piggy has been Matt's beautiful furry friend for many years. I have enjoyed watching their antics together and also being part administrator of her Facebook page. She's quite witty, a little philosophical at times, and always hungry!

I'm super grateful to my son, Matt, for giving great advice on this new book, for my step-daughter, Toni, for the lovely cover, and Michele Jones at AIW Press for publishing.

Please check out Piggy's Facebook page, Arcade Matt's YouTube channel and other socials.

https://www.facebook.com/iggythepiggycat

https://www.youtube.com/@arcade_matt

Piggy Finds a Home

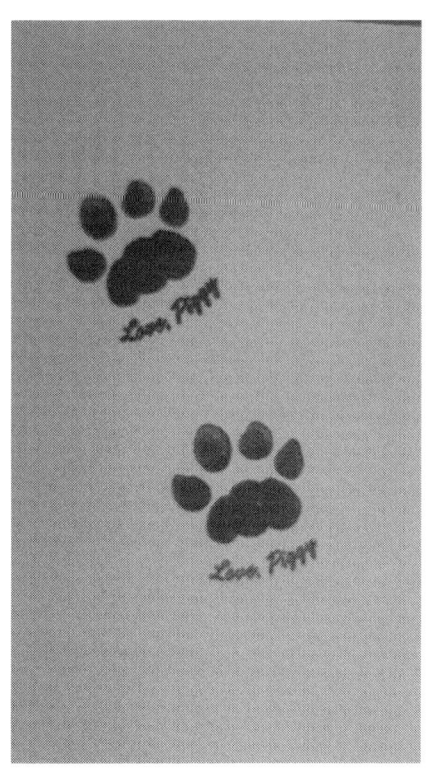

One

Sunshine filters through the screened window, warming my whiskers. I look over at Matt, blinking in the slow, lazy way cats do, showing him how much I adore him. I watch him at his most favorite of pastimes: computer editing. My adopted sister cat, Goober, runs amok--sliding on the hardwood floors, enthralled by a squeaky feather toy which has long since been silenced. She's a whirlwind of tiger-striped fur, young and vibrant. I'm a bit older, and more settled.

Goober jumps onto the windowsill gently prodding me with her paw-- her invitation to playtime. I look away. *Not now little sister.* I have more serious thoughts on my mind.

Last night, Matt found old paperwork while digging through a filing cabinet in his room. I watched several emotions cross his face as he studied the documents: sadness, and then anger.

"These are your adoption papers," he said to me. I peered over his shoulder and saw an old black and white photo of a cat looking back at me. I realized this was me a long time ago. "Muffin." I hardly remember the name and a shiver runs through me. I was so thin at the time. *Thin, neglected, and abandoned.* Another memory comes to mind, one I don't linger on too long: a hand raised in anger toward me.

Many years have separated me from that time. Years, and the love of one good man, my human, Matt. This moment is one of sweet, twittering birdies, crunchy tuna treats, and a fluffy, warm bed. I am a cat who is fortunate indeed.

"Piggy!" Matt calls out, and I shake myself back into the present. "Piggy, look," Matt says as he points to the computer screen. "You have over twenty-thousand 'Likes' on your Facebook page. That's quite an accomplishment." He walks over to me and scoops me from my perch, petting my head and scratching *the* spot behind my ears. Purr…my tail goes limp, paws tingling with ecstasy. Oh purrrr!

Twenty-thousand. Not bad for a cat who was once unwanted.

Matt sits back down, cradling me like a baby, and I snuggle into the familiar scent of his sweatshirt, safe in his arms. Goober crawls underneath the computer chair, tickling Matt's legs with her paws. He bends to pet her with the hand that's not supporting me, while the contented sound of my purring warms the silence of the room.

"You're a Facebook diva," Matt says, scrolling through the photos on my page. I have no idea what these words mean, but I consider them compliments because the smile on his face is huge and his happiness, evident. Picture after picture of such good memories: Matt and me making funny faces after a morning of play. Catnip-induced smirks upon the faces of my sister and I after a romp with new toy mice. My paw dipping into a dessert Matt left at his computer. Our little family.

I drift toward sleep, content on my human's lap, but the name Muffin once again comes to mind. And when sleep overtakes me, dreams and memories take me along with them.

The little girl found me shivering outside her house. Alone and frightened, I'd wandered out of the woods, still confused from the recent events that had led me there. Only a week before, I'd lost my human companion, the kindly old man who'd brought me into his home and then into his heart. His grown children had shown up one day and taken him from me. They said he wasn't fit to live alone any longer.

One of them tried approaching me, and I'd bolted straight out the front door and into the woods behind the house. That's where I watched and waited, scared and confused, hoping my companion would return. And when days had gone by with no sign of him, I resigned myself to the fact that I'd never see him again.

The little girl approached me and then picked me up. "Ooh, another kitty," she squealed. "Velvet's gonna love you." The child, grimy from many days' worth of dirt, brought me into her home. A place of utter chaos, a place where I would learn that the sting of a raised hand meant business.

I shivered, huddling in the corner of a damp, musty basement, the feel of cold cement underneath the pads of my paws. I had run to the sanctuary of the lowest level to escape the deafening sounds of the humans. A fight had broken out between the man and woman once again, and I knew to steer clear of them during these times.

I lay there looking over at the other cat, Velvet, who'd been my companion, my sister, through it all. She laid her head onto her paws and sighed, closing her eyes as if blocking out the tumult above.

My belly rumbled with hunger, and I crept forward to poke my paw at the upended plastic water bowl. Our food dish, an antique china saucer laid broken in two with the remnants of the last meal crusted on the edges.

Velvet looked up, her eyes huge and sad. I couldn't remember the last time we'd eaten. I knew she was hungry too, and I wished there was something I could do to comfort her. She counted on me, and I'd become her protector, motherly when she needed it most.

Sludgy water trickled slowly into a drain on the basement floor from a leak in the old washtubs. I moved forward to the puddle, lapping up the filthy liquid, and then retching it right back up.

I joined Velvet, curling next to her soft coat, and we both fell into fitful slumber.

When I awoke the next morning, I noticed there weren't any of the usual chaotic morning sounds. The humans were silent.

Weak from hunger and thirst, I could barely move. Velvet looked at me, sleepy eyes filled with questions.

I waited and still heard nothing. Curiosity got the better of me, and with the last of my strength, I mounted the rickety staircase, leaving Velvet behind. What I saw in the rooms above made my fur stand on end. The house stood in complete disarray. No sign of any of the humans. Closet doors stood open and empty.

They left us? I took a moment to process this thought. *Surely someone will be back.* I remembered talk of the woman threatening to leave the man and take all those kids with her.

I walked through the remainder of the place Velvet and I called home. Poking my whiskers into bedrooms, slithering into open closets, I could find nothing that gave a clue to what had gone on.

Back in the kitchen, I hopped onto the counter and found a skillet of cold, congealed bacon sitting on top of the stove. I called to Velvet and we both picked at the old, tasteless meal. Afterward, we washed each other's coats, and then curled together on the threadbare rug in the corner of the kitchen.

Several days went by with no sign of the family we'd lived with. I'd known fear before, but nothing had come close to the realization that hunger brought. My stomach rumbled constantly, and Velvet began to look thin and sickly. Looking to the sky one evening as I sat on the windowsill of the living room, I closed my eyes with a wish and a prayer and then fell into a dreamless sleep.

A rap at the living room window the next morning woke me, and the puzzled face of the mail carrier peered into the house. I heard him call out, "Hello, is anyone there?" I stretched out, reached up and scratched at the grimy glass with my paws startling him. "My goodness, are you alone in there, kitty?"

I yowled, scratching at the glass more feverishly. *Come on mister, what's it going to take? A neon sign perhaps?*

A few hours later, Velvet and I were scooped into cat carriers—something I still can't abide to this day—and escorted from the place we'd once called home. The mail carrier took us to a veterinarian's office. I heard him telling the girl at the front desk, "You shoulda seen the filth in that home. Stuff everywhere and not a drop of food or water for these two poor cats."

The days went by in a blur, doctors and nurses poking and prodding us, but there was plenty to eat and drink, and no shortage of cat kibble and fresh water.

When our health improved, we were taken to a shelter, Animal Friends, with a big sign on our cage: **Must be adopted together**. I'd heard the vet and his assistant talking one day: "These two can't be separated especially after all they've been through with each other."

Animal Friends was full of surprises. I'd never been around so many different varieties of cats, but there were other animals as well. Guinea Pigs squeaked in their cages, showing off their portly little bodies and whimsical skills. Bunnies scampered around their pen, their fluffy little cotton tails wiggling. The dogs were the most annoying of all. I didn't care for the constant yap, yap, yap of the wiry terrier nearby. When nobody else was looking, I let loose my best snake-like hiss to try and scare the "yip" right out of him, but to no avail.

A parade of people came and went, some pausing longer than others to look at me and Velvet. Hands poked into our cage--little kids with sticky- sweet fingers that smelled good enough to lick, and others that carried the scent of their own pets which I shied away from. Nobody appealed to me.

A big man with a kind voice came by one day. He spoke softly to me and Velvet and took time to read our sign. I heard him muttering something under his breath about misfits and rejection. When he reached into our cage, he stroked me gently, doing the same with my sister. All the while he kept talking to us, telling us what nice kitties we were. It didn't take him long to call the clerk over to let him know he wanted us. He could have picked Fiona, the prissy gray cat with the luxurious fur, or Sadie, the fetching blue-eyed Siamese. Surely there were many other cats there with gorgeous coats and darling personalities. I wasn't a stunning cat. As a domestic shorthair I'd always felt quite ordinary. I was shy and a little backward from all I'd gone through. But this man had seen something in me, something beautiful and valuable.

Of course I couldn't help but wonder if he might be like the others. Could we trust him? And if I liked him, would he also be taken from me as my first human companion had been?

The man turned out to be Matt's Uncle Rick who'd been looking for two cats to adopt. Since he worked with special needs children, he knew a thing or two about kindness and patience. He took us to a cozy home that night, and it was there I met Matt, his nephew, a skinny fellow with a warm smile.

The two of them stood looking at me and Velvet, plying us with tasty food, fresh water and an assortment of cat toys.

"I think the first thing we'll do, is to re-name you girls," Rick said.

He pointed to Velvet. "Your gray coat reminds me of a comic book character I always liked. I think we'll call you The Vision." Velvet blinked her golden eyes in response and sidled up to Rick.

"Now you," he said, indicating me, "I'm not so sure yet. Let's see if a name presents itself. How does that sound?"

I didn't care. Call me anything you want, but please don't call me late for dinner! I had developed a very fond relationship with food. I couldn't get enough. Bowls in this house were always filled to the brim with tuna cat chow. Treats were even more wonderful. When one of the humans took the treat bag off the counter, the crinkly sound would send me into spasms of kitty ecstasy.

Two weeks went by. Rick and Matt spent time with "Vision" the cat and me. Rick peered at me thoughtfully, a smirk lighting up his eyes.

"Well, I believe we've come up with a name for you," he said, patting my head and stifling a chuckle. "I think we'll call you Piggy. You have a pink pig nose, and well, er, you seem to have gained quite a bit of weight already."

Piggy indeed! Well, if that's what they wanted to call me, fine. Just keep the food and snacks coming, my friends, and I'd answer to anything.

Life settled into a pleasurable routine with these two young men. I enjoyed venturing into nooks and crannies in my new home. That is when I found that I bonded the most with Matt. His bedroom was in the basement, a small, low-lit room. I liked the cozy feeling in there, but mostly I liked Matt. He was a good sort, always in a happy mood with a nice, smiling face. He took extra time to cuddle with me or play, laughing whenever I did something he found amusing. Who knew that dipping my paw into the popcorn kernels in his snack bowl could be so funny or that his shoelaces would provide hours of entertainment for us both? Or that the paperwork he sometimes laid on his bed and the sound when I attacked it would be so hilarious to him? He was studying video editing and he began shooting videos of me and my antics.

Nighttime was my favorite--the soft blankets on Matt's bed, our special snuggle time and hearing Matt talk about his hopes and dreams for the future. I could listen to him for hours, falling asleep in the crook of his arm.

A couple of years flew by, and Vision and I were as content as cats could be. Something bothered me though. Vision had begun to lose weight once again. The spark in her eyes began to dim, and she slept more than ever. It was about this time that Matt took her to the veterinary clinic. They returned home a little quiet. Vision curled under our dining room table, unable to move, and hardly able to eat. I tried enticing her to play. I lay by her side, hoping she'd snap out of whatever was bothering her, but after a few weeks, I saw Matt take Vision away again. This time she never returned.

We'd been a team, inseparable. I wanted her back. I missed the lovely velvet cat I'd come to know as my sister. We'd been through so much together and now she was gone. With my heart broken, I reached out to Matt for comfort during this time, completely trusting him.

I awake, shaking myself from the long dream and memories, clearing my head. Matt gets up from his computer chair and lays me on his bed. Goober runs between his legs, making that little trilling sound when she wants to play. Matt chases her around the room while I sit watching them. Sticking my toes into the air, I begin licking my glorious white fur, extra careful to clean between the pads of my paws. Goober flies onto the bed, and I lay a paw over her back, pinning her down. I run my sandpaper tongue over my paw and wash cobwebs and dust from my adopted sister's coat. Who knows where she's been-- perhaps in the basement behind the furnace, poking her whiskers into places she shouldn't. Little by little Goober relaxes and begins to drift off to sleep, a content cat smile on her face as she relishes my grooming.

I glance over at Matt's computer screen, stifling a kitty chuckle. It's not easy being known as a Facebook diva and opinionated puss. It takes work, lots of work. Matt still films me, but in the last several years, he's been filming himself too. He's become a YouTube celebrity! His years of video editing and camera skills have paid off. Matt makes family- friendly arcade videos for children and their parents. He plays what he calls "claw machines" also known as crane games. You see them in arcades, in malls, and amusement parks--the big glass-encased games lit all the way around with sparkly lights, playing silly music and stuffed with prizes and plush toys. Matt purchased his own machine, and well, let me tell you a little more . . .

Matt and I moved out about a year after Vision went to the place that humans call the Rainbow Bridge. He'd grown older and wanted a home of his own. Although Uncle Rick had been wonderful, and we were both grateful for all he'd done, there was never a question where my loyalty lay. I was Matt's cat now and would be going with him.

The new house had even more rooms to explore and lots of windows with a panorama of outdoor activity for me to watch. Birds flitted from branch to branch in tall trees and then flew away, filling the air with songs. Colorful butterflies and striped honey- bees floated past, their erratic patterns almost dizzying. I sat on the windowsill in Matt's room for hours, late into the night, amused by all that nature offered.

The day the first arcade machine arrived, I thought Matt would burst with joy. An enormous truck pulled up in front of our home. I watched from the bedroom window as he greeted the man who got out of it. After signing several papers, they loaded a huge piece of equipment onto a wheeled dolly. I heard our front door open, and then hid under the bed for hours to escape the racket they made while they brought that contraption into the house. Later, when I emerged, curious and brave, I crept down the stairs to our game room and saw it. Matt shined the glass, tinkered with the electronic coin mechanism, and then loaded boxes full of small stuffed animals into the machine. He practiced on it for hours while I watched him, honestly a little indifferent to the whole thing.

"Piggy, this is our future," he told me.

I gave him a look. *I don't care about the future, Matt, just remember the present. I'm on a strict schedule here. It's suppertime, pal.*

Matt sat watching me. He asked if I was happy. I rubbed in and out of his legs revving up my best purr, hoping this would be the answer he needed. He told me there would be a surprise for me now since I'd been such a good girl. It would arrive in a few days. I loved surprises since they were usually in the form of a new toy, blanket, or tasty treat, so I waited with anticipation.

The big day arrived. Matt walked into the living room with a cardboard box. I sniffed the air, my delicate nose working, when an unusual scent caught my attention. The box began to meow, and Matt lifted a tiny grey-striped kitten from it. I backed up and hissed. *Uh, Matt, if this is the surprise, then I think I'd rather not.*

The new kitten was rambunctious and playful. I can't say I liked her much at first. But Matt knew me better than I knew myself. He'd sensed my loneliness and had seen how I thrived when I had another cat to look after--how motherly I'd always been. We named the kitten Goober, which is another name for little peanut.

Matt's YouTube popularity began picking up more and more. Families everywhere watched Matt's videos, even those living in other countries. He taught excellent tips on winning at the claw machines and other games, and with his fun, quirky personality, the people loved him. He filmed me and Goober too, always luring us to the camera with some zany stunt.

Fan mail and little gifts began pouring in. Kids would send drawings of the prizes they won. Nothing was better, however, than when the fan mail began to come for me! Little toys, drawings, and occasional bags of cat treats started to arrive. Matt decided to create a Facebook page for me, and his mom, Karen, who is a writer, started to post my thoughts and photos of my antics daily.

It's fun interacting with all the comments on my page. I like making people laugh and have developed a quirky cat persona as a food connoisseur. I am not opposed to a little humor regarding my girlish figure either. Many gentleman cats have tried courting me and approve of the way I look. I am living proof a girl doesn't have to have the perfect shape to have a slew of tomcats at her doorstep. I like a good meal, and I'm not afraid to talk about it.

I enjoy humor most of all and have penned a few poems in my day. I'd like to share my most popular one with you called:

Piggy's Ode to Food

Today I'm not quite in the mood,
May I just have a little food?
A little treat to tide me over,
A little snack for me and Rover.
Hey, I mentioned a dog, but we don't have one,
Oh well, why not, he'd be such fun.
I wouldn't care who came over today,
I'd share my food, we'd laugh and play.
So human, please don't make me sick,
Get me some treats, and be real quick.
You take too long, this cat is done.
So hop to it now, to the kitchen, run!
I'm waiting here with bated breath,
I'll fall over and starve to death.
Some crunchies please and I'll stop whining,
I'll sit at the table and I'll be dining.
Okay, enough, as you see I'm tired,
I've written too much and now I'm wired.
I'll let you know when it's time to eat,
Peace out, phew…now, this cat is beat.

There's so much seriousness in this hurting world. Matt and I like to think that if we can brighten just one day or at least a few hours for a child or her family, then we are doing something worthwhile.

The house is quiet, nighttime has fallen. Matt turns on the small lamps and nightlights in each room and a cozy glow surrounds us. We are in the living room now, and Matt settles into an overstuffed chair, his new video game system on his lap. Goober is washing, gliding a slender tiger paw over her face while I look over Matt's shoulder, watching a computer screen where colorful cartoonish figures jump around a make-believe landscape.

Matt shakes the treat bag sitting next to him, and Goober stops. Her little head pops up and she makes that cute cooing sound. I instantly come alert and meow my loudest just to be sure Matt doesn't pass me by.

I know better. I am treated like a special princess. I think about the less fortunate cats in the world, ones I see on other Facebook pages in the cat community. The ferals, blind cats, three-legged cats, and I pause giving a moment of thankfulness for who I am and where I am in this moment in time. Once neglected, abandoned, and unloved, I cannot help but feel gratitude for the circumstances that have led me on my journey.

I still miss my sister Vision, but I know I'll see her again someday at the Rainbow Bridge. There, we will frolic and play, and the tuna will flow freely. There, we will be reunited with other loved ones; our momma cats who we don't even remember now, and our litter sisters and brothers.

As I crunch into the treat, I look into Matt's eyes. What I see warms me to the tip of my pink Piggy nose. I see true, unconditional love.

Piggy Poetry

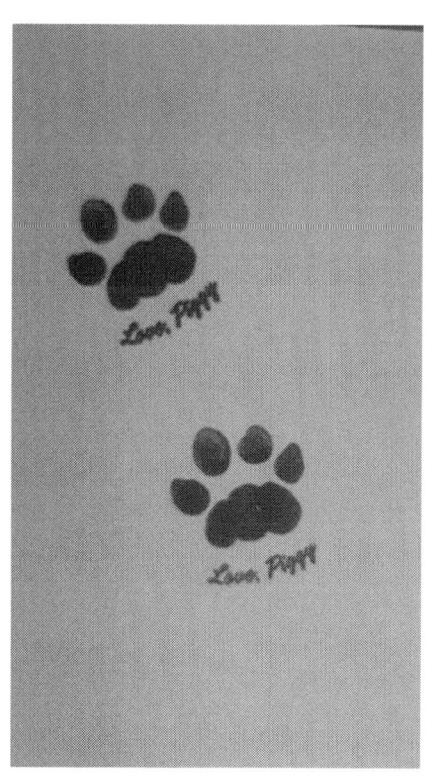

KAREN MALENA

My Favorite Place

The kitchen is the nicest place
åDon't I have the cutest face?
Treats and yummies here they come
Give me lots, but give me some.
Hurry please cause I'm a waiting
I don't want to be debating.
Thank you human for complying
Oh such goodies you've been buying.
Now it's time to have my feast
Hope your day is filled with peace!

Give Me Food

Here I sit inside the kitchen
For my food I'm truly itchin.
Human, open bags up please
Don't just stand and be a tease.
Give me tuna, give me chicken
Then my paws I'll be a lickin.
Salmon's also a good choice
Heed my meowing, hear my voice.
Okay, crunchies here I come
Peace out, love ya, Piggy's done.

Fishy Poem

Here I sit alone with dish
Can't I please just have some fish?
Tuna's best, I'm not complaining
A full belly I'll be gaining.
Make it quick and make it snappy
You want kitty to be happy.

Profound Piggy

So you know the saying, if a tree falls in the woods and nobody is around to hear it, does it make a sound... If a cat meows in the kitchen for her morning noms and nobody is around to hear, what should she do?

Meow

I am Piggy hear me meow
What I'm saying is feed me now
Human you'll just make me wait
What I need is a full plate.

Naptime

A little nap, a little doze
Until my rumbling tummy grows.
A little dream, and then I wake
To run to the kitchen, then to take
a little snack all just for me
Oh what joy, and oh what glee!

KAREN MALENA

Wake Up Matt

December

It's the first of December
So always remember
To be sweet and tender
To cats of all gender.
Make sure that their wishes
Are lots of filled dishes
With tons of good fishes
You know it's delicious.

Scratchin

I just can't reach to scratch this itch
My legs are trying to stretch and twitch.
A little help would be so nice
Let me give you some advice.
Humans, when your cat is trying
To scratch a spot, please be complying.
Get your hands and give it a go
Up and down our fur real slow.
Then we'll love you even more

Cuddle Me

Off to the Kitchen

A little rain a bit of sun
I'd really like to have some fun.
The human's gone and I'm a wasting
The food on the counter, I'd like to be tasting.
So join me if you want to please
There's ham, chicken SpaghettiOs and cheese.
I can be quick, he'll never know
He really seems to be too slow.
Just say the word, I'll be right back
There's too much food for me to attack.
Then later when my daddy's here
I'll whisper sweet purrs in his ear.
He'll never think I'd stoop so low
So off now to the kitchen I go!

Hot Dog

Chicken

They say it's good, it's finger lickin
May I just have a piece of chicken?
You left it out, so there's no choice
After all I have a voice.
It's like torture to observe from afar
Just run away human, and get in your car.
I promise to leave you tiny crumbs
I don't have opposable thumbs.
So there's no way to eat it all
Quick, Goober grab it, while I make him stall!
Alright, I'm playing, I'm only having fun
And now this cat's little "tail" is done.

Go Away Snow

I look outside and I see snow.
I yell at it, please away you must go!
I'm ready for birds, and chirping and fun
I'm ready for windows to be open, and run.
I want to feel warmth on my great kitty face
I want to enjoy all things at my place.
So winter, here's to you just leaving right now
Or you'll hear the wrath of my roar and MEOW!

Rain

Rain, rain go away
Little Piggy has to say.
It's no fun when skies are gray.
I can't frolic, I won't play.
In my bed all day I'll stay.

Ignoring the Human

There's nothing smarter than a cat
You know you can't argue with that.
A cat can sleep and play and then
Our master's voice we do pretend
To not hear and not respond
It frustrates you from here to beyond.
But don't you worry and do not fret
You will have the last word yet.
For cats are loving, sweet and kind
Always keep that in mind.
And when we hear the dinner bell
You never have to yell.
For we'll come running and we'll be there
Acting all perfect and like we care.
But we really do, it's just our way
Then we'll do it all over another day.

Weekend Fun

Now's the time for weekend fun
To your computer you must run.
For all the latest hype and gags
Hey, I don't want to brag
I just want you to keep on keepin'
With kitty love, just keep on heapin.'
All the smooches, all the kisses
This is what this Piggy wishes.
Have some fun, and try to play
Enjoy the weekend, enjoy the day
Now I wish you all the best
Phew, it's time to take a rest.

Piggy's Purr

I said a purr for you today
to let you know I care.
I said a purr for you today
and blessings everywhere.
Your friendship means the world to me
It's not too hard to find
A special thought, a little love
You're always on my mind.

Piggy Cleaning Goober

Goobie

I have a sis who's quite the cat
And crazy as can be
She spins on chairs
She climbs the walls
She's nuts as you can see.
But one thing that
You'll never find
My sister pointedly
Is not the purrfect cat I am
For there's only one Piggy!

Goober is Spidercat

Waiting for Daddy

At the bottom of the steps
sits a pretty little cat.
Alone with her thoughts.
If she could talk, she would say
something profound. Perhaps
something with meaning.
She sits and waits
for the human she loves.

Grumpy Piggy

Today I'm feeling a little grumpy
This bed, these blankets were too lumpy.
My precious sleep was so disturbed
And now I'm feeling quite perturbed.
This face, look at it, do you think I'm happy?
Why do you think I'm being so snappy?
But wait, you can remedy this situation
All you have to do is use some creation.
Head to the kitchen and fix me a snack
Now hurry, I'm waiting for you to come back.
Then you'll see a new Piggy, one that's content
No longer irate, nor continue to vent.
If I say please would it help you to move?
Oh, you think I'm being quite rude.
Well, next time you call me, just see if I hear
I'll pretend to be bored, I'll turn a deaf ear.
That's okay, I can hang with the best of the bunch
I'll just wait around until it's time for some lunch.

Dr Seuss Sheetz day

Every person in my town loves Sheetz a lot,
But only a fool who is grouchy does not
The grouch hates good food, and he gives no reason
Now please don't ask why but I think, this is treason
It could be perhaps that he isn't just right
Or maybe his pants and his belt is too tight
But I think the most likely reason of all,
May be that his stomach's two sizes too small.
Whatever the reason, the pants or the tummy
He needs to check Sheetz 'cause their food is so yummy.
There's fries, wraps and coffees all kinds of good stuff
I dare you to complain for I'll call out your bluff.
So head to your Sheetz for some really good food
It'll change even the grouches grouchiest moods.

I Can Haz Sheets

Halloween Cat

In time for your Halloween pleasure
I bring you a picture that's truly a treasure.
My sister with lamps for eyes to scare
A true kitty horror, you better beware.
For when cats are ready for Halloween treats
They do some truly amazing feats.
They howl and they yowl, they meow all night long,
Singing the tune of their people's song.
So if your kitty on trick or treat night
Tries to give you a spooky fright.
Just pick them up and don't be rough
Tell them okay, pussycat that's enough.

Goober Eyes Glowing

Time to Eat

A tisket a biscuit
Oh what can I eat?
Some Friskies or Whiskas
Just give me a treat.
When cats give that stare down long halls and bare rooms
Human, it's soon that you'll come to your doom.
So won't you please open a bag or a box
Forget your bare feet, there's no time for your socks.
Hop to it, come on, I've been waiting too long
Or I'll sing and I'll meow of my people's great song.

Warm Whiskers

Rain, rain please go,
I love the sun, I need it so.
We're tired of drip, we're tired of wet,
We need some warmth and we need it yet.
So give us that beautiful gorgeous sun,
So our human's can play and have some fun.
And all good kitties and all good cats,
Can look out windows, what do you think of that?
I love the feel of warmth on my whiskers,
I love to bask in the sun with my sister.
So if you decide to come back anytime soon,
I think we're all just gonna swoon.
I'm boycotting rain, just sayin, so please,
Give me a warm and wonderful breeze.
Okay, that's enough, my rhyme will now end,
As always, I thank you for being my friend.

Poem for Kindness

There are days that are great and the sun always shines,
And then there are others you see.
We feel kind of yucky and sometimes we whine,
But there's something that's helpful for me.
When I see someone hurting or see someone sad
The best thing that I found to do.
Is say something nice, and do something kind
Try to find ways to be helpful too.
Let's make the day better and make the day bright
By smiling, and saying good things.
We don't have to be loud and have to be right,
When we're nicer, the joy that it brings.
So take a few minutes and think of ways now
To do a good deed for a friend.
When you make time to be the best that you can
Then everyone wins in the end.

A Special Place

Do you have a place to go and dream
To think deep thoughts
Or so it seems.
That all your cares just wash away
In the glory of a bright new day.
Do you have a place meant just for you
Where beauty abounds and dreams come true
And every burden large or small
Appears to have no hold at all.

I am Queen

I am Piggy hear me meow
For this time I must allow
Human for you to see
All the splendor of me.
My fur is glistening
I hope you are listening.
I'm queen of this place
With my beautiful face.
Now come give me treats
Cause I wanna eat.
Enough of this adoring
I wanna go exploring
My food bowl you see
Come give it to me.
Thanks for your time
And enjoying this rhyme!

Go Away Snow

I look outside and I see snow.
I yell at it, please away you must go!
I'm ready for birds, and chirping and fun
I'm ready for windows to be open, and run.
I want to feel warmth on my great kitty face
I want to enjoy all things at my place.
So winter, here's to you just leaving right now
Or you'll hear the wrath of my roar and MEOW!

PIGGY THE CAT AND ARCADE MATT

Arcade Matt

Daddy and Piggy

Goober on Daddy's Head

Perfect Pose

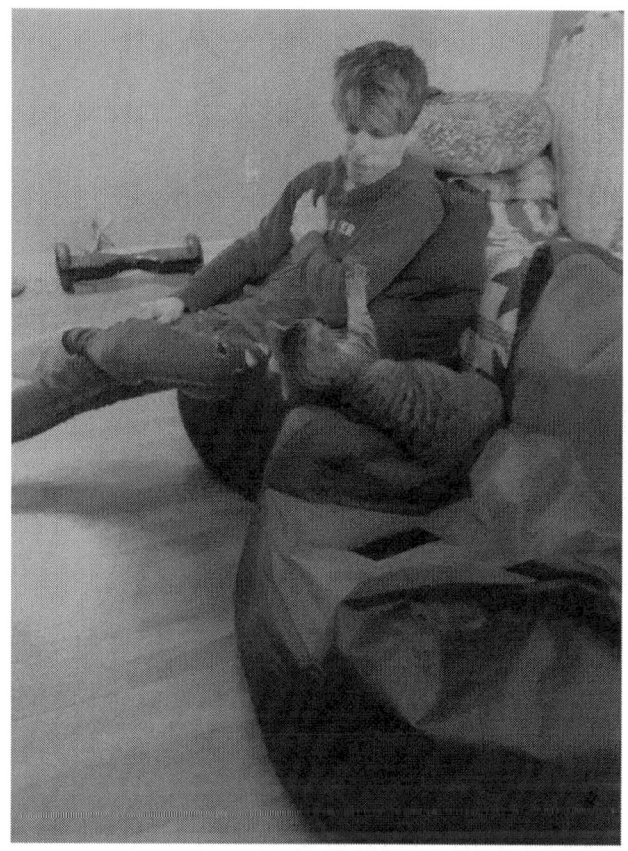

Goober Loving Daddy

Daddy and Cats

Hold Still Goobie

Me and Daddy

Big Smile

Funny Photo

PIGGY THE CAT AND ARCADE MATT

Hilarious

Goobie Bad Cats

I Beg Your Pardon

Goobie

Kissing Piggy

Matt and Cat

PIGGY THE CAT AND ARCADE MATT

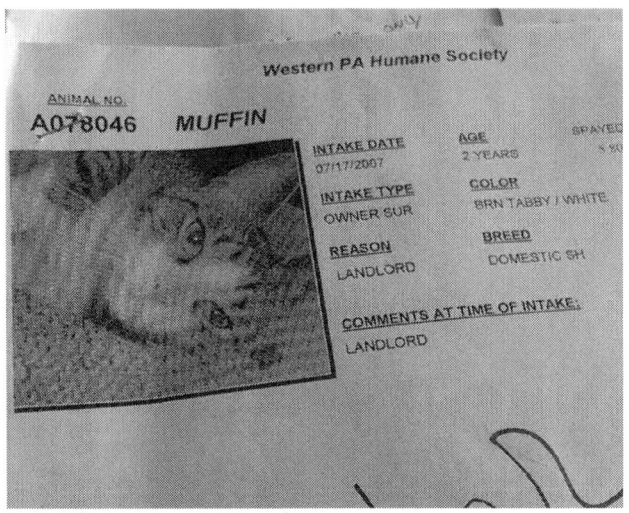

Piggy's Paperwork

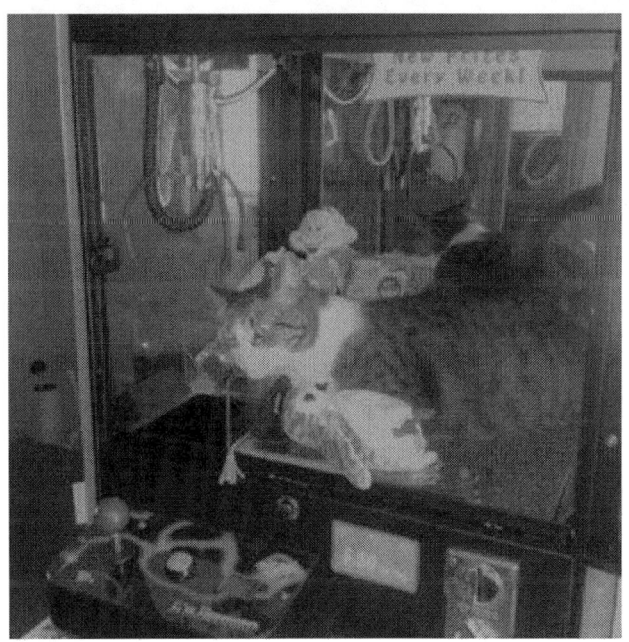

Piggy in Claw Machine

Piggy Loves Food

Purrfect

Sisters

PIGGY THE CAT AND ARCADE MATT

Hugs

Piggy's Big Adventure

Prologue

A dilapidated, gray-shingled house sat among tidy red brick homes in a quiet neighborhood of Ambridge, Pennsylvania. It stood out for the peeling strips of paint, the sagging front porch, and the tendrils of ivy creeping up the side. A wooden fence badly in need of a paint job surrounded it with a creaking, rusty gate. Behind this gate sat the meanest, toughest, and angriest cat anyone ever laid eyes on, his name was Bolivar. He belonged to no one, and nobody belonged to him. Day after day, he'd wait for unsuspecting prey, seducing them with his snake-like voice, and then grabbing them when they least expected.

The house in which he stood sentry had been deserted for several years. He claimed this property for himself and picked fights with other cats in the neighborhood who dared step foot inside his weedy yard.

Bolivar lifted his ragged orange head and licked at a wound on one paw. The scar on the right side of his face and his partially torn ear pained him today, the results of many battles. His stomach growled; he hadn't eaten a decent meal in at least four days.

Recently, the neighbors had begun to lock their trashcans up tightly; a few of them included heavy bricks on top to prevent him from tipping them. Not a scrawny bird to eat, not even a tasty little crawling bug; his mood went from bad to worse.

Out of the corner of his eye, through one of the slats in the fence, Bolivar spotted movement. In the next yard, a plump, furry brown mouse frolicked about. With his changing luck, Bolivar perked up. He lay low to the ground, every muscle in his body tense and alert. His tail twitched in anticipation and his hind quarters wiggled as he sprung forward to pounce upon the unsuspecting rodent. . .

One

Piggy the cat basked in the kitchen window's sunlight at the home she shared with her human. Bathing herself, something caught the corner of one eye. Her whiskers twitched as the prey eyeballed her. Its beady little eyes glowed in the early light, a small morsel of food clutched in his tiny claws. Her tail thumped, once, twice. As if some kind of signal, the brown furry mouse dropped the half-eaten crumb of Zesty Dorito chip and scurried into a tiny hole in the wall.

Piggy strolled over to the remnant of its morning meal, sniffing at it. *How dare him!* She thought. *My human's precious snack food.*

Slowly, without making a sound, Piggy crept forward to poke a furry paw into the crevice where the hateful prey had entered. She sniffed the air, her well-tuned sense of smell catching the scent of the quarry. *I'll teach that vermin a thing or two. I'll show him who the boss is.* Little by little, she inched her paw further into the hole in the baseboard.

The rodent stood with his back against the wall, his breath coming in shallow gasps. His belly rumbled and he put a paw out to quiet it. *Only half a crumb. I'm going to have to do better than that.* The evil feline paw entered the front of his home, searching, scratching. The mouse knew he was lucky this time; thank goodness the cat hadn't seen him a minute or two sooner. . . He shuddered.

After what felt like eternity, the white paw retracted. Melvin, the mouse waited for ten, fifteen, and then thirty minutes. He poked his head back out of the hole and glanced around the room. Quietness had settled over the house and as he sniffed the air, the scent of cat was gone.

Melvin scrambled onto the kitchen counter his nose to the air, whiskers working. At last he was rewarded with an open bag of animal crackers. Scooping one out with his tiny claws, he sat munching the vanilla cookie while watching for the hated cat.

Piggy curled up on her human's bed. Distressed over the filthy little mouse, she vowed to find him later. *Nobody steals Matt's food.* Her human, Matt, who was oblivious to the scenario which had just gone on, spun around from his computer and scratched Piggy under her chin. Piggy closed her eyes as she enjoyed the attention. She began to purr and drifted off to sleep. Her last thought was *I'm coming for you mousy. Just see if I don't.*

Piggy awoke the next morning, forgetting all about the mouse. The one thought, above all else, her most favorite in the world: food. She stretched her body, and a yawn escaped her. Matt was still asleep, his arm flung across his face. Piggy prodded at her human to try and annoy him into waking, but to no avail. Her stomach gave a rumble, and she tried harder, pawing at feet this time. Matt rolled over, and one eye opened peering at her.

Ah, good. Let's get this show on the road, Matt. I'm hungry.

PIGGY THE CAT AND ARCADE MATT

Piggy sat at attention, her food bowl almost empty. Matt walked by her, grabbing a granola bar from the kitchen counter. He ran down the stairs to his bedroom in the basement area of the small home he shared with his Uncle Rick. She heard him getting ready for work, the sounds from below of the usual and customary morning routine. His hairdryer snapped to life, and Piggy scrambled from the kitchen to the safety of the living room couch; she tried to wedge her chunky body underneath as far as she could. The sound of that machine grated on her nerves. Once she'd been curious while it was lying on his bed, coiled like some sort of snake about to strike. But later when Matt turned it on and she felt the whoosh of hot air coming from it, she ran as fast as her stubby legs could carry her and hid for the rest of the day.

The sound of Matt's feet on the stairs brought her out from under the sofa. She resumed her position at the food bowl looking at Matt, and then looking into the bowl. *Human, feed me, and be quick about it.* Didn't he see she only had a small ring of crunchies rimming the bowl? He'd be gone for hours and then she'd starve. Starve! A cat has to eat. *What's he waiting for?*

She tried the hypnotic stare all cats are famous for. Nothing. Okay, when all else fails. . . Piggy produced a yowl that could curl her human's hair. Matt stopped before heading into the bathroom for a final check on his blow-dried hair. "Piggy, what's your problem?" He turned to her.

If I had thumbs, Matt, I'd point. What do you need, a sign? Another yowl and then another hypnotic stare.

"You had your morning food already," Matt laughed. "You don't think you earned that name for nothing, did you?"

Okay, now he's insulting me. Fine, I don't need you anymore. I'll just try to jack some food from the counter when you're gone, Matt.

"You be good, and try not to get into any trouble today, okay?" Matt patted Piggy's head, scooped his keys up, and then he was gone.

Piggy strolled over to the dining room window and jumped onto the ledge looking out into the backyard. *Trouble? Who's he kidding? I'm so bored and lonely.*

Vision, I miss you. Piggy sighed. Thoughts of her sister, Vision the cat, crept up on her. Vision, who'd been so sleek and beautiful, so healthy and playful, had been gone now for over half a year. The two had been the best of friends, protective of one another; as close as two cats could be. They shared toys, food, and bathing rituals. Vision even saved the last of her treats for her sister late at night. They'd been found abandoned in a home together. A kind-hearted person rescued them by bringing them to Animal Friends, a wonderful shelter. They were nursed back to health and adopted into a good home with Matt and his uncle.

When Vision began feeling poorly, Matt took Vision to the v-e-t-s. She came home with medicine, and it seemed to be helping her at first. A second visit came almost a week later but Vision never returned. At first, Piggy hadn't understood why her beloved sister was gone. She hadn't understood why Matt and Rick looked so sad. Then it had hit her: Vision was never coming back.

I wish I could go outside, Piggy thought. *There are so many neat things outside this window: flying birds, colorful butterflies, tall grasses swaying in the breeze. I'd give anything to be out there. My sister would have loved to be an outdoor cat...*

A scratching sound brought her back to the moment: scritch, scratch. Surveying the room, she spotted Matt's most favorite item: his prized claw machine. He'd saved up money for months to buy it. It was stuffed with silly-looking plush toy animals and assorted riff raff. Piggy didn't understand why humans enjoyed these machines so much. Matt even had another small stack of plush toys spilling from a cardboard box next to the claw. Her gaze drifted to a small purple toy bear which was moving. Piggy jumped down from her perch just in time to see the mouse she'd spotted last evening tugging at cotton stuffing poking from the bear's side.

Piggy wasted no time; she ran as fast as she could, swatting at the rodent with her paws. At first the mouse produced a muffled shriek, and then he dropped the cotton wadding which had been stuffed partially into his mouth. He looked around, frantic beady eyes darting to and fro. Piggy stood between him and his mouse hole. He scurried underneath the dining room table looking back over his shoulder. Piggy was right on his trail. The opening at the bottom of the claw machine was only a few tiny steps away and the mouse scampered up into it.

Piggy stopped short in front of Matt's machine. *That silly mouse ran up inside! At least now I have him trapped. Oh, you just wait Mr. Mousy. This Piggy's coming for you.*

Piggy stood on tiptoe looking through the glass. The brown mouse climbed over a large, plush banana. He slithered over a bright green snake. He disappeared under a pile of yellow rubber spiky balls. Piggy had seen enough. The mouse was trapped inside, and she would make him pay. Lowering herself onto the floor, she peered up into the prize chute of the machine. All of a sudden it seemed like such a long way up. Several toys had fallen into the area of the chute and Piggy dug in with her claws, pulling herself up, up, up into the crane machine. If that silly rodent could do it, she could too. Piggy reached the top a moment later and began pawing around digging for the mouse.

She succeeded in knocking more plush toys into the opening of the machine. The more she dug, searching for the mouse, the more toys tumbled into the slot. The mouse was nowhere to be seen. Just then, she heard the sound of metal clanking and realized while she was digging in the pile of toys, the little critter scampered right back down the prize chute and slipped out the bottom. He stared at Piggy, a look on his face of defiance and stuck his tongue out at her.

"Ha! Serves you right, silly puss," the mouse said, his beady eyes alight with mischief. "Fooled you, didn't I?"

"You just wait until I get out of here," Piggy threatened. "You'll eat your words, and then I'll eat you."

The mouse gulped, and Piggy could see she'd struck a chord with him. She crept to the tunnel she'd climbed through and stopped. The opening at the bottom of the machine lay several feet below. The walls of the prize chute were metal and slick, and she was suddenly aware of her limitations as a cat. She tried inching her body back down toward the opening. Her sharp claws scratched and slipped on the metal surface to no avail. It was then that panic settled full bloom in her stomach: she was trapped like a rat, no pun intended. Matt just couldn't find her in there; he'd be furious.

Piggy pawed at the glass and meowed loudly, then louder, and finally, the loudest she could. The mouse stood several feet in front of the machine. "Help me!" Piggy meowed. "Get me out of here!"

It appeared as if the mouse struggled with his conscience. As he prepared to run from this scene, he turned back toward the sound of the frantic cat.

"Give me one good reason I should try to help you?" Melvin backed up several steps, all the while looking at the struggling cat trapped in the claw machine.

"For one thing, I'm afraid of being closed in. For another, I have to use my litter pan!" Piggy yowled and danced a crazy jig, scratching at the glass at the front of the machine.

"Why can't you just climb down the way you got in?" The mouse walked a few steps closer this time. He stood on two legs with his arms crossed in front of him.

"I can't do it, silly mouse. It's too far down that hole and I keep slipping. Don't just stand there. *Help meeeeeowww!*"

The mouse sat back on his haunches and began howling with laughter. "As I see it," he said, "if I rescue you, you'll owe me a favor." Melvin wiped his tears from laughing so hard.

Piggy stopped scratching long enough to think about the situation. There was no way she was getting out of this machine without help;

yet she didn't want to owe this creature anything. "Well don't just stand there; what's your plan, rodent?"

Melvin appeared deep in thought. He ran back and forth in front of the machine, his industrious mind working. At last he spoke.

"I have an idea." He scampered up the sideboard near the claw machine and began rooting through the small box of coins Matt kept next to it for guests to play.

"This isn't the time for stealing shiny coins," Piggy whined. "I need out of here!"

"That's what I'm about to do," Melvin said. He grabbed onto a quarter, and like a small acrobat, climbed down the piece of furniture to begin scaling the side of the claw machine.

Melvin stood at the front of the machine teetering on the edge near the coin slot. He and Piggy stared at one another through the glass eyeball to eyeball.

"I want your word," he said. "I want you to leave me in peace to snatch food whenever I want. I don't bother you, you don't bother me. I'll have you out of there in no time if you trust me."

Just then Piggy had her own brilliant idea. "Hmmm, let me think about this. You think you're a pretty good thief, do you? Well, then I have other terms to this little arrangement. You help me get extra food and snacks and you have a deal."

"Done!" Melvin said. "Now, listen cat, I'm going to put this coin into the slot. That starts the claw moving. When I jump on the button of the joystick, you position yourself under the claw. See up there?" He pointed to the dangling metal object above Piggy's head.

"What on earth?" Piggy asked. "You actually think you're going to snag me with that thing? Then what? I tumble out of there like some sort of prize?"

"Precisely," Melvin said. "The extra toys that fell into the prize chute will cushion your fall. You'll be fine. Now get ready."

Piggy didn't like this one bit, but the mouse did have a point. Into the machine the coin clinked. Melvin jumped onto the joystick and pulled at it with all his might. The claw began moving with a whir. Piggy watched in horror as it rose above her.

"Wait a minute," she shrieked. "What if it doesn't hold me?"

Melvin appeared to have not heard her. He guided the joystick with all he could, and then pressed the button as it hovered above the fearful cat. The claw dropped down near Piggy but snapped at air bringing up nothing.

"Let me try again." Melvin scurried down the machine, back up the piece of furniture which held the box of quarters. This time he snatched three of them and made his way to the front of the machine.

Piggy realized she'd have to embrace the spirit of cooperation, as this was the only way for her to exit the machine. She tried making herself as available as possible for the claw to grab her.

A coin clinked into the machine; Melvin drove the joystick with all the force he could muster. Again, it came up empty. A second quarter dropped in and nothing happened.

Melvin was panting by this time, his body exhausted from all the work. "I don't think I can do this," he said. "I'm so tired."

"Come on," Piggy coaxed. "Give it your best shot. We can do this together, me and you. It'll work this time. I can feel it."

Ushering all his strength, Melvin climbed the joystick once again after depositing the third quarter. Piggy stretched up on tiptoe as far as she could for the claw when she felt it clutch around the middle of her body. Up, up into the machine she went, dangling from its grasp. All of a sudden, she was airborne for a moment when the claw let go of her and she tumbled down into the prize chute and out the door.

PIGGY THE CAT AND ARCADE MATT

Melvin scuttled down the machine as the cat lay there in a heap of plush toys.

"Thank you little one," Piggy said, standing and shaking herself off, a bit worse for wear. "Good job."

"We haven't been formally introduced," the mouse said. "My name is Melvin," and he took a little bow.

"Piggy at your service"

The two shook paws, Melvin's tiny hand was almost swallowed up in the big, furry paw of the chubby cat.

"Wait, oh, wait," Melvin giggled. "Stop that," he said as Piggy began licking the fur of Melvin's back.

"Thank you again," she said. "Matt wouldn't have been happy seeing me stuck in there. I guess that was pretty stupid of me."

"Well, if it wasn't for me. . ." Melvin put his head down.

"Nonsense. It's okay now and as soon as I use my litter pan, I'll meet you in the kitchen for a snack. All that excitement made me hungry. We'll see how good you really are at stealing food."

"Ha ha, this is delicious," Melvin said as he and Piggy shared a bit of sandwich Matt had left on the counter. Piggy pulled at the tasty slice of ham wedged between soft slices of Italian bread; she liked the salty taste of it. Melvin nibbled the edges of the crust.

Piggy sat in amazement over the ease in which her friend could climb cupboards and wedge his tiny body into the smallest of openings. Melvin was able to push items from shelves that Piggy would never be able to reach.

"I can't believe all this food is ours for the taking," Piggy said. "There's times the bowl of crunchies Matt gives me barely satisfies me. You're going to be a great help."

"Aw, thanks Piggy," Melvin said sitting back on his haunches. His fat, furry belly looked ready to pop from the portion of sandwich he'd eaten. "I've always been good at snatching treats."

Piggy finished eating and ran her tongue over her paw, washing her face and whiskers. She licked the fur between her toes, nibbling at a ragged nail.

"What else would you like to do today?" Melvin asked. He'd gotten his second wind and scampered around poking his nose into other rooms.

Piggy waddled into the living room. "I'm ready for a nap," she said. "All this excitement wore me out." She walked over to the couch, stretched her body to its full extent, and clawed at the armrest a few times.

"Psst, Piggy, over here," Melvin gestured with paw and tail. "Look, the stuffing's poking out of this one." A hideous lime green stuffed bird with bright orange feathers had tufts of its cotton innards sticking out from a tiny hole in its side. It was one of Matt's claw machine wins.

"I could use some new bedding in my home," Melvin said as he pulled at the cottony stuffing, laying bits of fluff on the carpet. "Help me, please?"

Piggy shook her head. What an unusual companion. A little high-strung, a little excitable, but she'd been missing her sister more than usual; perhaps Melvin would fill the void.

She walked over to the bird and held it down with her paw as her new friend worked. When Melvin seemed satisfied with the pile, he and Piggy began carrying chunks of it to his home in the wall.

Melvin lived beyond the baseboard of the small dining room. Piggy crouched low to the ground trying to peer into the hole. She could see Melvin's feet scurrying around, hear him fussing as he moved his miniscule furniture around. He'd gathered some interesting items from all over the house. A spool of thread served as his table, and a small box which had once held some matches made the frame of his bed. An empty can turned on its side housed bits and pieces of food he'd taken.

"Nice place you have there," Piggy said and yawned. "I'm awfully tired though, Melvin. I had quite the busy morning. Perhaps we can get together a bit later, okay?"

"Fine, fine," Melvin said, rearranging furniture for the third time.

Piggy hopped onto the couch to knead at a soft afghan with her paws. Before long, she was fast asleep.

Piggy awoke to the sun slanting at a different angle through the partially open, slatted blinds. It must be late afternoon. *How long was I asleep?*

Melvin was nowhere to be seen. Piggy stretched and her belly gave a growl. Hmmm, getting hungry. She hopped from the couch and padded into the kitchen. Jumping onto the counter, she threw the last of the morning's sandwich to the floor. A cupboard door was partially open. Standing on tiptoe, she tried reaching for an open bag of Doritos.

Melvin appeared rubbing sleep from his own beady eyes. "I can get them, just wait for me." He ran as fast as his little legs could carry him and brought them each several of the crunchy treats. They munched in silence for a few moments, enjoying their food.

Melvin gave a little squeal of delight and climbed the counter once again. A bag of donuts sat off to the side. He nibbled a small hole in the bottom of the bag.

The sound of a key turning in a lock startled them. Melvin scurried to his hole and Piggy lay upon the last crumbs of sandwich, hiding them beneath her body.

"What on earth?" exclaimed Matt. He walked into the dining room to view what was left of the day's adventure. "What happened in here?" The room was a mess, toys and several other items from his claw machine still spilling from the hole.

"Holy cow," Matt said aloud. He looked over at his cat. "Piggy, what's going on?"

Like I'm going to answer you. Piggy blinked at her human in that charming way she always did then pretended to ignore him.

Matt walked into the kitchen. "I thought I put these away," he said, grabbing the bag of Doritos from the counter and placing them back in the cupboard.

"What's this under you?" Matt scooped Piggy into his arms, kicking at the remnant of sandwich. "Piggy, were you jacking food in here today?"

Piggy began purring. *If you only knew, Matt.*

Matt brought Piggy into his room, and she snuggled in his toasty warm blanket. He sat back at his computer to immerse himself in whatever it is that humans do. Out of the corner of her eye, she saw Melvin outside the room. He was dancing from foot to foot trying to get her attention. Piggy glanced over at Matt. He seemed intent on staring at random pictures of other humans, occasionally hitting the pad in front of the screen. Piggy shook her head and pointed with one paw. Just then, Matt looked over at her and she pretended to wash her leg. With toes pointed into the air, she blinked at her human and washed and washed. Melvin must have seen Matt turn, for he was no longer outside the room.

"That's strange," Matt said, getting up and peering outside his room. "Something caught the corner of my eye. I'm starting to think we have mice in here, Piggy." He shivered. "I noticed a hole in the bottom of the bag of donuts too; time for you to earn your keep and catch the darn thing." And then, almost as an afterthought, "I gotta tell Uncle Rick."

Piggy jumped from the bed, leaving her human. Melvin stood on the basement stairs.

"Are you crazy, Mel, Matt could have seen you. Actually, he thinks he did see you. You must be more careful," Piggy whispered.

Ignoring her, Melvin danced a little jig on the steps. "Piggeeee," he squeaked.

"*Shhhh!*" Piggy cautioned. She motioned for Melvin to go upstairs.

"*Loookeee* what I found!" Melvin brought Piggy near his hole in the wall. A bag of shiny, multi-colored marbles lay on the ground. "I love pretty baubles." Melvin said. "They were under Uncle Rick's bed." Melvin dug through the glass trinkets and came up with one that was sky blue.

Piggy yawned. "That's nice, but next time, I hope it's something a bit more exciting."

She would eat her words. In the next weeks and months, Piggy and Melvin would become more involved in events that would be anything but boring. Her quiet, neat little world would turn upside down.

Two

"You have to watch the house, Piggy," Matt said to her as he grabbed an overnight bag and loaded it with jeans, t-shirts and other essentials. He zipped his laptop into its special carrying case.

"Uncle Rick will be here to keep an eye on you. You'll be okay," Matt placed his things onto the couch. He walked into the kitchen one last time, checking Piggy's food and the extra cat treats he laid out for her.

"I'll miss you, Piggy," Matt said as he scooped her into his arms. He planted kisses on top of her furry head while she wriggled to get out of his grasp.

Okay, okay, enough already, Matt. I get the point. Leave now please.

Placing his cat on the couch, Matt patted Piggy's head one last time, hoisting his overnight satchel onto his shoulder. With a final look around the living room, he left the house, closed and locked the door. The turn of the lock resonated with finality.

Piggy jumped from the couch to knock at the wall near Melvin's home: nothing. She rapped again but to no avail. There was no sign of the mouse: not a whisker, not a view of pink ear or his long, skinny brown tail.

That's odd. He's always here this time of the day.

Crouching down, Piggy peered into his hole the best she could. His neat little room didn't have a thing out of place. His bed was made up, his stash of food stacked in little rows in his tin can. Puzzled, Piggy sat back on her haunches until the tiniest sound emerged from outside the window. Tap, tap went the sound. *Scritch, scratch.*

Piggy jumped onto the sill of the dining room window to investigate. Her mouth dropped open in surprise; Melvin sat upon the ledge on the outside of the house.

"Melvin, what on earth?"

"*Pigggeeee!*" Melvin squeaked as he jumped up and down like a miniature jack-in- the-box, and then scurried back and forth, doing a happy dance. "You and I can get outside the house."

"How on earth?" Piggy asked. "Where?" "Head downstairs to the laundry room. I'll meet you there from the outside."

Curiosity overcame Piggy and she flew down the steps two at a time, running into the laundry room. Piles of Matt's clothing lie folded in a brown wicker basket. Any other time she'd rummage through the comfy-looking clothes, but there were more important things at hand now. Piggy looked around waiting for the signal from Melvin.

Just then his tiny head poked through a screen high upon the window on the wall. "Lookie! There's a tear in the screen." He pushed the rest of his body through and now stood inside.

Is it possible? Will I be able to leave my human's house to roam freely outdoors as I've always wanted?

"How did you find this?"

"I was running around last night down here looking for some dryer lint for my bed. I felt a little breeze rush into the room and voila! I found the opening."

"Melvin, you amaze me."

"Jump up, Piggy, come on," Melvin coaxed from high upon the wall.

Piggy sprung onto the dryer and scattered socks and a box of spring fresh dryer sheets. She crouched and sprung again and landed on the sill of the window this time. Melvin held the screen for her while she wedged herself through.

Once outside, Piggy stared in awe at the surroundings: bushes, flowers, and grass. So many things she'd seen from inside the house as she pined looking out the windows. It was all there, waiting for her and Melvin to explore.

The sounds were the most wonderful of all: birds, birds and more birds chirping away in the trees. The warm spring day tantalized Piggy, and she knew what true bliss felt like.

Piggy ventured into the front yard. She'd never seen so much color in one place before. Scores of small yellow flowers poked their bright heads through the soil. Nearby, purple flowers intertwined with them, making a beautiful contrast. Winged, airy butterflies darted to and fro in the air, some lighting on the blossoms for a moment before fluttering off to another. Piggy watched in fascination as it appeared these small angels drank from the delicate blooms. On the grass a wiggly brown worm slid along, barely making time in its slowness.

Piggy crept forward and poked her paw into a mound of dirt where hundreds of small black ants bustled about, some with tiny crumbs of food on their backs as they disappeared into a hole at the top of their little mountain.

Her eyes followed the flight of a bumble bee that buzzed near her face. Piggy swiped at it with her paw; it hovered near for a moment and then flew off to busy itself in the middle of a bright red flower.

No wonder humans enjoy being outside so much. How could you ever get bored out here?

Piggy had been so completely absorbed in the surroundings she'd forgotten about Melvin. She needn't have worried; he lie on his back with his legs crossed; a small blade of grass clutched in his tiny paws; staring up into the sky with a wistful look on his face.

"Piggy," he began. "Have I ever told you about some of the dreams I have?" He didn't wait for her to answer. "Yeah, once, I was a mouse in shining armor in King Arthur's courts rescuing cute little rodent damsels in distress. In another one, I was a swashbuckling pirate aboard a huge ship bound for treasure in a faraway land."

Melvin threw the blade of grass to the ground and laced his hands behind his head. "Another time I flew high above cities with a superhero cape billowing out from behind me. Yessirreee, I sure like my dreams."

"You watch way too much television," Piggy said. "I see you lurking around when Uncle Rick is watching all of those crazy movies. I don't like them."

"Piggy, do you know what your problem is?

You don't know how to have fun."

"Mel, I just don't see myself as a superhero type. I like my feet planted firmly on the ground."

Melvin jumped up then. "Piggy, let's play make believe. Wouldn't it be fun to have the type of adventures that I have in some of my dreams? You could be Super Pig, and maybe I could be Melvin Mousketeer."

Piggy rolled her eyes and climbed the steps of the front porch. She perched on a ledge to observe farther out into the yard. "Melvin, just for a moment, could you stop and smell the flowers?"

Melvin jumped up and ran over to a yellow bloom. Whiskers working, he pulled it down to his nose. "There, I've smelled the flowers." Yellow flecks of pollen stuck to his face.

Piggy almost fell off the ledge laughing. "Silly Mel, I didn't mean literally. You know what I'm talking about." She raised her face to the sunshine to bask in the warmth. "I'll play pretend with you in a little bit."

With Melvin, there was no such thing as patience. He had hyperactive mouse disorder and never stopped moving. Piggy could sit in the same spot for hours to soak up the warmth and comfort of a good blanket, and now the warm sunshine.

Melvin picked up a small twig and started slashing the air with it like he was wielding a sword. "Take that," he said, "and that." His little weapon dotted the air again and again.

"Oh, all right then," Piggy said and got up to stretch. A discarded cardboard box sat next to the porch, and she sharpened her claws on it, ripping it to shreds.

"Okay, Melvin, who would you like me to be?"

Melvin stopped his swordplay and jumped up and down.

"Great, Piggy, that's more like it. Here, you be Super Pig." He ran to the side of the house and returned a moment later with a ratty old dishtowel Matt must have thrown into the garbage at one time. He tucked it into Piggy's collar so that it resembled a cape.

"What superpowers am I supposed to have?" Piggy glanced around and hoped that nobody was watching.

"Piggy, you my friend can fly!" Melvin cried. "You can fly, and you can see into houses with your x-ray vision, and you have the strength of ten cats."

"And what, pray tell, are you going to be?"

Melvin looked down for a minute. "I'm going to play the bank robber." He looked up with a sneaky expression on his face, a miniature copy of a bad guy in an old B movie.

"Okay, Piggy, I'm gonna pretend I just robbed a bank." Melvin took off and raced away through the side yard and around back. Piggy galloped after him, her magnificent cape billowing behind her.

Melvin cowered underneath an old plastic chair in the back yard.

"Hmmm," Piggy said. "Let me see if my awesome vision helps me to locate the perpetrator." She scanned the yard pretending to search for Melvin. "Aha, there he is!" Piggy pounced gently upon the alleged thief and picked him up; she placed him behind a slatted piece of wire that housed a few small bushes.

"Let me out!" Melvin cried. "Oh, someday you'll get yours, Super Pig." He stomped his foot and crossed his arms in front of him trying his best to project a menacing look. Piggy burst out laughing. "Melvin, you've missed your calling. You belong on a stage or in the movies."

"Thank you, thank you," Melvin said, bowing. A robin flew by overhead and lighted on a branch high up in the neighbor's maple tree. "Cat, cat, cat," he called out.

A cloud passed over to blot out the sunshine.

A slight breeze picked up and Piggy shivered. "Silly birds," she said.

"Piggy, I have something else to show you. Come see what I found." Melvin jumped up and down and tugged at Piggy's collar. The makeshift superhero cape fell onto the grass. Melvin ran ahead of Piggy into the neighboring yard. A trash can lie on its side, food spilling from it: McDonald's containers and wrappers with a partially eaten hamburger, bits of a sausage muffin and scrambled eggs.

Piggy's eyes widened. A feast! As she approached the smorgasbord, a strange hissing sound stopped her short. The yowl and mewing of some horrible creature made the hair on her body stand up. Melvin, who'd been ahead of her, paused and crouched low; a sinister beast approached from under a hydrangea bush. The muscular orange tabby advanced upon them with sharp, pointy fangs bared.

Just then, a huge whir of brown fur tore past them. Piggy ran for cover from the huge dog which took chase after the orange tabby; Melvin scampered onto her back holding on for dear life. Piggy and Melvin managed to make it back into their own yard while the sounds of growling and hissing filled the air around them.

The dog's ferocious barking went on and on; Piggy tried to squeeze back through the hole in the screen to the safety of her basement. As she was part way through, and while Melvin stood shoving against her for help, they both froze as the sound of a creature clearing its throat made them pause.

"Ahem," the sound went again. Piggy wriggled out of the hole, her fur stuck up in every direction, her back alert with tension from the huge dog that stood near them. A snake-like hiss emanated from her mouth. Melvin's eyes widened, and though he wanted to run, his little feet were frozen to the spot.

"*Hellooo young'uns,*" the dog began. "Bolivar's gone for now. There's no need to fear."

What's this? Piggy hissed again. She'd never been this close to a dog.

Before them stood an enormous German shepherd; his ears and tail were black, but his muzzle was graying. Piggy realized in an instant that this fellow was old. He shook a little as he spoke, and his voice quivered a bit.

"You can stop that silly hissing, Missy," the dog said. "Old Bolivar and I go back a long ways. Yep, me and that stupid cat have us a pretty big feud going on." The dog chuckled to himself as if it was a private joke meant only for him.

"I'm sorry to be so rude. The name's Sargent Rolf Whitaker retired K-9." The German shepherd saluted the two creatures before him with a shaky paw. "Been livin' in this here neighborhood, oh, goin' back a ways now, maybe ten, twelve years. I'm originally from Mobile, Alabama."

Piggy found her voice. "I… I've never met a canine before. You must forgive me for staring. I thought dogs and cats were natural enemies, you see." She extended her paw and the two shook. "I'm Piggy and this is my friend, Melvin,"

Melvin, fuming, sputtered, "No, no, no, this is not going to work. Being friends with a cat is one thing for me, but a dog? *No way!*"

"I'm sorry about Melvin," Piggy explained. "He's a bit protective of me as you can tell."

"Well, I'll be. . ." Sargent Rolf said, blowing out a long breath. "As I see it, cats and mice don't usually get along."

"You said the cat's name is Bolivar and that you two have a rift of some sort going on?" Piggy changed the subject.

"*Yessirree*. Me n' old Bolivar, well, we've been feudin' for a long time. He's a right bad one, he is." Rolf motioned to his back right leg. It was then Piggy noticed a huge chunk of his flank with no fur. Ugly pink scar tissue rimmed the area.

"Did he, uh, did he harm you?" she asked.

"I didn't see it comin'. One day I was out patrolling my back yard when that demon cat sprung out a nowhere and dug in, bitin' me to high heaven. He had a grudge from way back when I was a lot younger; had a pretty bad infection there for a while from his ugly fangs. My human got me all fixed up though."

Piggy sniffed at the leg, while Melvin tugged at the fur of her underbelly.

"Well, we must be going," Melvin said. "One of our humans might be coming home soon. Piggy would be missed." And he shoved against his friend, trying to push her away.

"Thank you for saving us from that cat," Piggy said, ignoring Melvin. "That was very brave of you."

Just then, she felt a huge, wet tongue slurp the side of her face.

"Quit it," Piggy said, giggling. She wiped a paw over her face as the dog grinned before her.

"Y'all are very nice," he said. "Hope to see you again sometime." Rolf stood at attention and after another quick salute, was gone.

Later that evening, after Matt's uncle went to sleep, Piggy knocked at Melvin's hole in the wall.

"Psst, Melvin, you awake?" She waited for what felt like eternity when Melvin finally emerged, rubbing the sleep from his glassy little eyes. A huge yawn followed, and Piggy could swear she saw teensy tonsils.

"It's late, Piggy," Melvin said crossing his miniscule arms in front of himself and stamping one scrawny foot. "You disturbed my dreams."

"I thought you might like a snack," Piggy said. "I have something special planned."

Melvin stood with his arms folded looking like the world's tiniest mouse statue.

"Fine, go back to your comfy bed and your stupid dreams," Piggy said turning away. "I'll eat by myself."

"I thought maybe you didn't care for me anymore. After all, you found a new friend today."

Piggy turned back. "Oh Melvin, is this what it's all about? You think I'm choosing a dog over you? You have nothing to worry about. Stop being jealous! Come see what I have!"

Piggy padded into the kitchen while Melvin trudged behind her. He stood on his back legs, nose pointed into the air, his keen sense of smell at high alert.

Piggy wedged her body behind the stove, inching something out little by little. A hidden can of SpaghettiOs emerged on its side, half-full.

Melvin's eyes lit up. "Where did you find this?" He couldn't contain his glee and ran circles around the can.

"Matt must have heated some for dinner one night and forgotten about it," Piggy said. "When he went to sleep, I knocked it from the counter and pushed it behind the stove. I'm pretty good at thievery too you know." Piggy motioned for Melvin to eat.

Like a shot, Melvin ran and buried himself inside the can. Piggy could hear the chomping of his teeth as they devoured rings of pasta. Melvin backed out of the can and Piggy began pulling pawfuls of little 'o's and meatballs onto the floor. She licked the sauce and gnawed at the pasta with gusto.

After a few moments, Piggy sat back, cleaning the sauce from her whiskers, and washed her paw over her face. Melvin scrunched his small frame into the can one last time. He backed out a moment later, a half-eaten piece of spaghetti clutched in his tiny paws. His brown fur was matted with sauce. The can of SpaghettiOs sat empty on the floor.

"Come here," Piggy said. "Look at you." She began to lick Melvin's back, washing him with her tongue and paw. He rolled around, giggling. "Stay still. Your fur will dry with all that sauce stuck in it." The light flew on in the kitchen. Matt's Uncle Rick screamed. "I knew we had a mouse!" He grabbed at the broom behind the kitchen door, swatted at Melvin, and missed Piggy by a few inches. Piggy picked Melvin up in her mouth and ran from the room. She deposited him under the living room couch; Rick poked and prodded with the broom underneath cupboards and the refrigerator.

"Did you get it, Piggy?" he asked, wielding the broom like a giant weapon. Piggy rubbed against Rick's leg and began to purr. "We'll have to get an exterminator in here." Piggy stopped rubbing and almost choked. She flew into the living room and whispered a plan into Melvin's ear.

Minutes later, she returned to the kitchen where Rick stood drinking a glass of water. In her mouth she carried what appeared to be the dead body of a mouse. Rick's eyes widened and he backed up a step, grabbing for the broom once again. Piggy laid the body of Melvin at his feet, while he kicked at it with one socked foot. When the mouse didn't move, Rick seemed satisfied. He took the dustpan and broom and deposited the body into the trashcan.

"I'll get that out tomorrow morning," he said, switching off the kitchen light and returning to his room. "Good job, Piggy." He patted her head.

Piggy waited near the trash can, her heart pounding in her chest. When Rick's door closed, she tapped at the can and Melvin emerged no worse for wear. He scampered down the side of the can and clutched the sides of his body from laughing so hard.

"We fooled him, didn't we, Piggy?"

"Yes, good performance, Mel. But we must be more careful in the future. Hopefully he'll forget about wanting an exterminator. You must never be seen again."

The two friends curled under the sofa, Melvin resting in the crook of Piggy's arm while the two of them drifted off to sleep.

Three

Matt returned from his time away with scores of empty cardboard boxes. He lined them up near his room in the basement as Piggy watched from a perch on the stairs. *What's he up to?*

Matt's uncle descended the basement stairs. "So, two weeks is the big day, huh?"

"Yep," Matt answered. Gotta really start packing now." Matt scratched his head looking around. "I accumulated a lot of junk through the years." He chuckled, opening a box and began to throw random items into it.

Rick cleared his throat. "I, uh, think we have mice in here. Piggy caught one last night."

"Oh yeah, I thought I saw something a while back but forgot about it with this move and all. I never thought buying a house and getting ready for the big move would be so stressful. I've had so much on my mind." Matt stopped loading the box and noticed Piggy for the first time.

"Yep, it'll be me and you, Pigster," he said, using his nickname for her. "We're gonna strike out on our own."

Piggy thumped her tail on the stairs and looked from Matt to his uncle. They were moving? That's what this was all about? What on earth would she do about Melvin?

That night, when all was quiet, Piggy talked with her friend while they sat together on the windowsill of the dining room.

"He said what?" Melvin asked.

"Yes, my friend, I'm afraid so," Piggy said, sighing the way cats do. "Matt's been planning this for some time now. I think his uncle said two weeks."

"Piggy, I'm scared. You can't go. I don't want us to be apart." Melvin scampered onto Piggy's back nestling into the fur around her neck. His tiny whimpers cut into the silence and shattered the peacefulness, breaking Piggy's heart.

"Listen to me, Mel, it's all set. There's nothing I can do about it. Matt must have been making plans for months now." Melvin crawled around the front of Piggy's body and she licked the soft fur of his back, her rough tongue making it stick up like quills. The crying stopped.

"I-I've seen the boxes all over the place," Melvin said while another sniffle escaped. "I wasn't sure what was going on."

Piggy sat back, thinking. She and Matt had been together for about five years in the home they shared with his uncle. Piggy had been content where she was, but another side of her, the adventurer, longed for something more. Could she give up her best friend now?

Piggy jumped down from the sill, Melvin still clutching onto her, and she placed him onto the floor in front of her. Melvin buried his face in the fur of her underbelly, small sobs racking his body. She put a paw around him, careful to keep the claws retracted. "There, there, friend, please stop crying. I've been thinking of some things you know."

Melvin stopped his caterwauling and looked up. "A p-plan," he hiccoughed. "Piggy, did you come up with a plan to bring me to the new house?"

"Melvin, he has boxes thrown around all over the place. All we need to do is find a small one, load your household items into it, and hoist you in; Matt will never know. It can work. I know it can." Piggy sat back quite proud of herself for concocting this intricate scenario. *Stealth Piggy, I'm ready for anything.*

Melvin cheered up instantly. "Do ya think so? Do you really feel it will work? I can't be away from you, my friend, I just can't."

"As I see it, Mel, we have about a week and a half. Matt's so busy getting his stuff ready, he won't notice you and I bustling around. Besides, tonight he's at his friend's house playing poker. Come on." Piggy led Melvin to his hole in the dining room wall. She crouched outside as he scampered into his cozy little room and watched as he began piling thimbles, matchboxes, and other items into one corner.

"I wish I could help you," she said. "My paw can't reach. . ."

"I've been meaning to clean up a bit in here anyway," Melvin said, tugging at an old, discarded handkerchief he'd found on the basement floor one day. "Maybe I'll even find different stuff at the new place."

"That's the spirit, friend," Piggy said.

Tears forgotten, Melvin was in organizational mode. He made his way down the basement stairs practically skipping as he spotted the piles of boxes. Many of them were open, contents poking from them. Others were taped shut with thick, clear tape and some even had writing on them.

"Here's one," Melvin motioned for Piggy. "See, I can crawl up into this and scatter my belongings way down the bottom."

Piggy stood on tiptoe peering into the box her friend had chosen. In it was an array of old video games, belts, greeting cards and a couple sweaters. "I guess this is as good as any."

At least two hours went by with a trinket or piece of Melvin's collection in their clutches. The friends trudged back and forth from Melvin's home in the wall upstairs to the open box below. His favorite item, a discarded non-working pocket watch was hauled out last.

"Do you know how much time I spent polishing the brass on this?" Melvin asked. "And look," he pointed to the tiny roman numerals on the watch's face. "Let's be very careful with this, Piggy."

It took both of them to pull the watch to the bottom of the box; Piggy inside and Melvin holding onto it, guiding it forward. When they had everything stashed as far down as it could go, they sat back admiring their work.

"This calls for a celebration," Melvin said. "Let's go find something wonderful to eat." The two made their way back upstairs; Melvin poked into cupboards until he spied a half-eaten crumpled bag of vanilla wafers. He pulled at them and they crashed to the floor; the clip that held the bag shut skittered under a cupboard.

Piggy dug in first to enjoy the sugary snack. Then Melvin settled in to crunch on his own delicate biscuit. Crumbs littered the area around them while Melvin continued to stuff his cheeks with the precious morsels.

The rattle of a key sounded in the front door, and Melvin scurried to his empty home in the dining room. Matt walked in; his arms piled high with a few more boxes.

"Hey, Piggy, what are you up to?" Matt set one of the boxes down and leaned down to tickle his cat under her chin. She did her best to initiate a purr, smiling at him with the half-smile all cats are famous for. Matt, apparently, was too pre-occupied to notice the crumpled, now empty bag of vanilla wafers near her. Piggy swooshed her tail a few times, and the bag disappeared under a cabinet.

"You ready to move next weekend?" Matt opened the refrigerator and poured himself a tall glass of milk. The aroma made Piggy's mouth water; she clawed the length of his jeans reaching up.

"Ouch. No, you can't have any," Matt chuckled, as he drained the glass in a few swallows and peeled Piggy's claws from his pants. He placed the empty glass into the sink, and Piggy made a mental note to lick the remnants from it later.

Later that night, it hit Piggy: the realization that she'd be leaving the only home she'd ever known and loved. She poked into upstairs rooms she hadn't visited for a while. She sniffed furniture, couches and chairs to commit to memory the scents of her old life. She looked around at the décor of the home, her sanctuary, and felt a bit melancholy to let go, regardless of the prospect of a new, exciting life on the horizon. Piggy laid down on the soft, fuzzy blanket on the couch to let sleep overtake her.

Piggy woke up the next morning, as the first hint of dawn crept into the sky beyond the living room window.

A tapping sound startled her, rhythmic and annoying. She hopped from the couch to try and find where it was coming from. From the corner of her eye, she spied Melvin as he tapped an old pencil against the glass of the dining room window from the outside. Piggy jumped onto the sill.

"Come on out, Piggy," Melvin squealed. "It's a great day for an adventure."

The last of the nighttime creatures, other small rodents, a possum, and several raccoons scampered about in the remaining darkness. Curiosity overtook her, and Piggy made her way downstairs, past Matt's closed bedroom door to the tear in the screen, her gateway to the outdoors. Pushing her body through with a slight bit of effort, she found herself on the outside of the house once again.

It was lighter and her nocturnal vision easily adjusted to the surroundings. She slipped through the hedges that bordered the houses and spied Sargent Rolf, nose to the ground, pawing at something in the dirt. Melvin wasn't anywhere to be seen, but it didn't cause Piggy any worry . . . yet.

"Good morning, Rolf," Piggy said walking over to the dog.

"Well, good mornin' Missy," the dog answered with a huge doggy grin on his face. "What brings y'all out here so early?"

"I have only a few days before we're leaving," she said. "My human is taking me to a new house. I guess my friend Melvin wanted to escape to the outdoors before we go."

"Sorry to see y'all go. I just met you, but I want to wish y'all well."

Just then, a loud series of squeaks filled the air. "Melvin!"

Piggy turned in all directions to try and find out where the sound came from. Squeeee! Squeee! It went, followed by a low throaty chuckle. Bolivar!

Rolf stopped digging and cocked his head sideways. "Over here," he said as he ran out of his yard and into the alley behind their houses. He stopped short with Piggy at his heels. There, before them, old Bolivar stood. One paw clamped over Melvin's tail. The other dangled inches from his frantic head.

"Piggggeeee! Help meeeee!" Melvin cried as he tried to run. It was no use; the cat had claws extended and the tail of his prey was trapped.

"Let that mouse go this instant!" Rolf barked. "You do as I say, Bolivar."

PIGGY THE CAT AND ARCADE MATT

The orange cat snickered. He batted at his prize a few times. "Let go of this tasty morsel? Never." He picked Melvin up in his mouth and scaled a huge oak tree which stood between the abandoned house he lived in and Rolf's yard. Rolf pawed at the bottom of the tree to try and shake it with his massive paws. Bolivar slipped neatly out of sight, dropping to the ground on the other side of the enormous fence that partitioned the old property.

When Bolivar hit the ground of the old house, Melvin tumbled out of his mouth. Shaken for a moment and breathing hard, Melvin had seconds to think before the cat pounced upon him once again.

An old porch sat before him with crooked stairs leading up to a torn screen door partially off of its hinges. Melvin saw a slight opening at the bottom of the door. He breathed deeply and realized that the cat would never be able to find him in the house, without hesitation, he took off like a shot headed for the crack under the door.

Melvin scaled the stairs as quick as his little legs would allow, not risking a minute to turn around and see where the hated cat might be. He slipped under the inch high opening of the door and found himself in a stale, musty, and darkened room.

Moments later, an orange paw wedged itself underneath the door to reach and search. In the dim light, Melvin could see the razor-sharp claws extended. He breathed a sigh of relief for the first time since he'd been taken.

"Mr. Mouse," the cat crooned. "Come on, I won't hurt you. I'm just playing a little game, that's all."

Melvin moved away from the door and adjusted his eyes to the darkened room. The heavy curtains were drawn against the light of day; the furniture in the room was covered with sheets and blankets, and they looked like hulking ghosts in the dimness. Thick dust covered everything, and Melvin sneezed once, and then another time.

"It's no use," the cat said. "I will find a way into this house. And when I do, you're mine."

Piggy, where are you?

Melvin hopped onto a chair nearest one of the windows. Parting the curtains a bit, he looked out into the yard. His friend would be worried sick about him.

Piggy tried scaling the tree as the tomcat had done, but she'd never climbed anything like this before. She realized her limitations as a house cat and began to cry. "Oh my poor Melvin, my sweet little Melvin. Oh what can we do, Sargent?"

A robin flew by then chirping out a warning: "Cat, cat, cat." He landed on a branch high up in the oak tree to observe the scene below.

Piggy ignored the incessant chirps. If only she could get over that fence, she'd rescue her friend before it was too late.

"Corporal," Rolf saluted the robin in the branches of the tree.

"Sargent," the bird saluted with one feathery wing. "What's going on in the neighborhood, sir?"

"It seems ol' Bolivar here snatched up my new friend Piggy's wee mousy. Can you see what's going on beyond the fence?"

The robin viewed the fenced yard and scanned it with his excellent vision. "Yes sir. I see the perpetrator. What shall I do boss?"

Rolf appeared in deep thought when at last he spoke. "There's no time for me to be diggin' under the fence for a rescue. I wonder if you would round up some of the birds and critters in the neighborhood to grab the wee fella."

"Yes sir." The robin began calling out. "Help friends. Help is needed." In just minutes, several species of birds began flying in, sparrows, cardinals, blue jays gathered in branches of the tree. Many of them eyed Piggy suspiciously, but as the robin explained the situation, it appeared that they were ready to help.

Squirrels chittered and ran down from high in the tree; a huge raccoon waddled into the yard with her baby clinging to her back.

Piggy couldn't believe her eyes. So many birds and other creatures had put aside their differences at the dog's command. She stared with admiration at Rolf.

"Can you see the mouse?" Rolf asked. Several birds shook their heads. One small barn swallow, a shy fellow who'd flown in a little later, said he'd seen the mouse run to the safety of the house. The cat appeared to be alone now and was pawing at the front door of the old home.

"I got a plan," Rolf said, as he motioned for the birds to gather near.

"I'm not standing by that cat," a blue jay said, pointing one bright blue wing at Piggy. "I don't trust any of them."

"Nonsense," Piggy said. "You don't need to be afraid of me. I just want my friend back." She started to sniffle.

Rolf put a paw out on Piggy's back. "Don't worry yourself any. I've been in much worse situations."

"We're gonna distract that ole tomcat you see."

Bolivar heard a noise behind him. Turning around to scan the weedy yard, his excellent cat vision saw nothing. He resumed clawing at the door of the house. No sound from inside, but not to worry: the mouse would be in his belly by noon.

Scritch went the sound once again and then the scamper of tiny feet. Bolivar spun around to see a blue jay and robin pecking in the high grass. They'll be my dessert, he had time to think before something dropped on his head. Plunk went another small, hard object and then another. Bolivar stepped back to witness several squirrels in the rafters of the front porch. They bombed him over and over again with chestnuts and acorns.

As he was being distracted by several of the silly squirrels, he failed to notice the chain of animals lined up near the latch at the fence in front of the yard. Squirrel stood on squirrel, their feet balanced on the others' shoulders. More birds flew into the yard now; the sound of their beating wings loudly disrupted the morning stillness.

"Over here, cat," one of the birds motioned for Bolivar to catch her. He took off, flying from the porch just as the latch was drawn at the gate. Rolf, tall and stately, stood outside with Piggy at his heels.

Bolivar spun around at the sound of the squeaking gate. "No!" he screamed, baring fangs and letting loose a hiss which sounded more snakelike than ever.

"See if you can find a way into the house," Rolf whispered to Piggy as she walked past Bolivar, head and tail high in the air. She didn't give him a second glance.

Bolivar hunched his back, the matted, orange fur sticking up as prepared for battle against the hated German shepherd.

Melvin heard the plunks of the acorns and chestnuts hitting the front porch. He had no idea what the sound was. He hunkered into a corner of the dark living room as a spider scuttled nearby.

"*Yessss, yessss,*" the arachnid said. "*Me seeees a mousssiiieee.* Come, let's be friendsss."

Melvin screamed and ran from the room with no idea where he was going. Daylight shined through a small crack several feet in front of him; Melvin realized that he was in a small kitchen and the light poured from a splintered back door. Just as he was about to exit the house, a feline paw wedged itself through the door. Oh no, not again, Melvin thought but the voice on the outside this time stopped him short.

"*Melviiinnn!* Mel, where are you?"

It was Piggy. Somehow, someway, she'd made it into the yard to save him. Melvin squealed with delight.

"*Pigggeee*, I'm here! Stand back and I'll try to scoot out the crack."

With every ounce of strength, Melvin pushed his body through the crevice until his little head poked out on the other side; he was met by the rough sandpaper feel of his friend's tongue. He'd never been so happy to see her.

Bolivar and Rolf glared at one another in the front yard. The raccoon, squirrels and birds stood nearby waiting for Rolf's command. Bolivar advanced and the birds pelted him with their wings, flew around him, and gave Rolf the advantage that he needed. The raccoon waddled forward, pulling Bolivar's tail. He cried out and backed away.

"You're finished here," Rolf said. "I don't want to hurt you. Leave now, and never return."

"Have you forgotten who's got the better of whom?" Bolivar asked, as he licked a wound on his paw from a nasty nip one of the squirrels had given him. "It is I who hurt you, mighty hero. Never forget that." Bolivar slunk away as the animals gave cheer.

Piggy and Melvin made it into the yard as the birds swooped around; squirrels slapped one another on the back. Rolf sat by, his doggy tongue lolling from his mouth, a huge grin on his handsome face.

"What'd we miss?" Melvin asked.

"Our Sargent came through again," squeaked one scrawny squirrel. "He's a legend around here, ya know."

Rolf hung his head. "I'm no legend. This time it was y'all who deserve to be congratulated."

"Rolf, what do these animals mean by legend?" Piggy asked.

"You never heard tale of Sargent Whitaker?" the raccoon questioned. "He's a war hero from Afghanistan. He saved his trainer and platoon."

"Aw, shucks," Rolf said. "Any of you'd have done the same."

"He got a purple heart," a squirrel spoke up this time. "He doesn't like to talk about it, but he's a big war veteran from way back. He saved my babies one time from Bolivar too."

"He saved my nest of eggs once," a female cardinal chirped in.

"He saved his human too," another bird said. "That's enough, friends," Rolf said. "I'm just glad we rescued this here mousy from the clutches of the evil one. Y'all go back to your homes now. We can save the tales for another time."

One by one, the animals began to go, leaving Piggy and Melvin alone with Rolf.

"How can I ever thank you enough?" Piggy asked.

Just be my friends," Rolf answered.

Melvin ran up to the big dog then, hugging him around his huge, muscular leg as much as his little arms could.

"Thank you," he said. "I'm glad we met you."

The day of the big move arrived. It was a Sunday, and Matt woke up early to finish up the last-minute packing before his brother and a few friends would arrive in the moving truck.

Piggy had to be very cautious; Melvin stood outside his hole in the wall to try and blend in. Once, when Matt ran outside, Piggy hoisted Melvin onto her back and flew down the stairs, ready to toss him into the box they'd chosen for his home items. As she reached the bottom, she noticed a small box had fallen over onto its side. Cat treats and some of her toys had been stashed in this one. But what caught her attention was the partially open bag of catnip. There was no way Piggy could resist.

The pungent scent assaulted her sensitive nose and as she caught another whiff of the heavenly aroma, in one quick swoop, she grabbed the bag onto the floor. With Melvin forgotten about for the moment. Piggy frolicked and rolled, her juices flowing as the catnip took effect. Wobbling around and looking for her water bowl a few minutes later, she spotted Melvin standing nearby with his arms crossed in front of him, stamping one little foot impatiently.

"Couldn't stay out of the nip, I see," Melvin said, shaking his head. "Tsk, tsk. This is no time for silliness, Piggy. This is serious business."

Piggy shook herself off, her senses a bit dulled now; she'd have to be more careful.

She picked Melvin up to try and toss him into the box.

After two failed attempts, Melvin tumbled to the bottom of the box. Piggy rubbed her eyes with one paw as her vision doubled.

She sat off to the side to watch and wait. She tried to commit this particular box to memory, so she'd have no trouble locating it at the new place.

The sound of heavy footsteps in the rooms above alerted Piggy that the helpers had arrived. Melvin's voice squeaked out one last time, "See you soon, Piggy."

All around, chaos began. Boxes were picked up, furniture was heaved around, and the young men worked together.

"I'll be back for you in a minute, Piggy," Matt said, as he brushed the hair and sweat from his forehead.

Another wave of catnip delight passed over Piggy. She dropped to the floor, wriggling.

"Hey, Matt," one of the movers, Matt's friend Dave, asked. "What about this open box?" He indicated Melvin's hiding place. Piggy perked up a bit.

"Oh, that's throwaway stuff," Matt said. "I'll put that out near the garbage can when we're almost done." Matt and his friends disappeared back up the stairs.

Throwaway? Heart pounding, quite sober now, Piggy wasted no time. "Melvin, hey, Melvin," she cried as she jumped onto the top of the box to peer into its depths below, paws frantically digging past bits of junk. Two tiny, beady eyes glowed in the darkness.

"Are you crazy, Piggy? They'll see you." "Listen, would ya? They're not taking the box you're in. I heard that they're using it for trash."

"*Squeakers!*" screamed Melvin; he scurried out of his hiding place and climbed the contents of the box to jump out as fast as his little feet would allow. Just then, Dave rounded the bend of the stairs to pick up another box. He saw the mouse at the last moment and dropped the box he held onto.

"Matt, there's a mouse in here!" He stomped and danced a crazy jig to try to hit the mouse which scampered furiously about. The two other helpers ran down the stairs and laughed at their friend.

"What, a little mouse gives you the willies? Come on, Dave, we gotta finish packing up this truck."

With a look back over his shoulder, Dave piled the spilled contents into its container once again. He climbed back to the first floor of the house and left a confused Piggy and Melvin to decide what to do next.

"What are we going to do?" Melvin cried. "My stuff! All my things and my precious pocket watch!"

"Melvin, there's no time to worry about that now. We have to get you into another box." Piggy looked around and knew that she had only minutes before the movers would be back. Catnip had dulled her senses. She should never have gotten into it. Piggy spied another box taped partially shut. She studied the shapes of the letters on the box. It looked like this, *STUFF FOR THE NEW HOUSE.*

"Mel, let's try this one," Piggy said as she motioned for Melvin to hurry.

The mouse stood near the box which housed his life's inventory. Unwilling to part with his things, he crawled back in and tugged on his watch. "Piggy, help me!"

"It's too late," Piggy cried. "Mel, they'll be back in a few minutes!"

With a downcast look, Melvin emerged with one final glance into the box of his beloved items. Piggy motioned to the new box once again, and she began to chew and claw past the pieces of tape which held it together. Melvin dove into the small opening she'd created, just as they heard footsteps once again.

This time it was Matt, and he held the hated cat carrier in his hands; the torture device which had brought Piggy to several veterinary visits. She tried to slink away.

"Oh no you don't; come here, Piggy." Matt's hands lifted her off the ground and placed her into the mini hotel on wheels. It had soft pieces of blanket on its floor, several cat treats, and her favorite squeaky toy.

As Matt locked the door after one final look around the house, he placed Piggy's carrier on the sidewalk. A clinking sound startled her, and Piggy saw a man walk Rolf past their house on a leash. Rolf stopped at the door of the cat carrier and his nose pushed through the slats.

"Come, Rolf," the voice of his owner said. "I'm sorry," he said to Matt. "He really likes cats. He won't scare your kitty." He tugged at Rolf's leash.

Matt laughed. "I don't think my cat's ever seen a dog before."

Silly Matt. Piggy touched her paw to the nose that wedged itself further into her carrier. "Be well, Piggy," her canine companion whispered.

"You too, friend," she said as they were pulled apart.

Once Piggy was lifted into the car, she decided it wasn't for her. Meowling over and over again, she hoped to annoy Matt. *You try it, Matt; see if you like being squashed into a small space.*

The drive wasn't long, and twenty minutes later Matt pulled Piggy's carrier from the car and placed it on a sidewalk in front of a small brick home.

So, this is the new place, Piggy thought as she watched through the opening in front of the carrier. A few leafy bushes grew in the front yard, and small, neatly trimmed trees. Hedges bordered the home and small yellow flowers.

I think I'm going to like it here. Piggy felt herself being lifted into the air. She was brought into the house, up a flight of stairs, and placed into a small bedroom on the second floor. Matt opened the front of the carrier and left the room after closing the door.

The sounds in the rooms below frightened her, and Piggy cowered in a corner as much as the small space would allow. Thoughts of Melvin and worry over which box he was in played at her mind.

The door to the room flew open several minutes later. It was Matt. "Piggy, you okay?" The soothing sound of her human's voice brought Piggy out of the corner.

No, I'm not okay. I'm scared to death if you really want to know.

Matt stroked her fur. Reaching out into the hallway, he brought in new ceramic food and water bowls. "I'll be back for you in a bit." As an afterthought he added, "Oh, I made you a fresh litter pan too." He placed a new pan with fresh-smelling crystals against one wall.

Well, aren't you the best, Matt?

When the door closed once again, Piggy took a step towards the new food bowl. At first, she tentatively placed a paw into the crunchies to stir them around until the scent of tuna drove her crazy. She dug in, a nervous wreck, and ate so much food her belly ached.

After using the new litter pan, Piggy jumped onto a small windowsill that faced the front of the house. Matt's friends were bringing a few more boxes into the house. She tried looking for a box which had the writing she'd seen earlier. She didn't see it.

Piggy jumped down and curled herself into a ball. She placed a paw over her head as if to blot out the day and all the newness around her. She fell into a fitful sleep.

When she woke up, the sounds in the rooms below had quieted down. She worried for Melvin once again. Poor little guy, he couldn't be happy stuck in the bottom of a strange, dark place.

Matt returned and Piggy strolled past him, the natural curiosity of a cat. She poked whiskers into another upstairs bedroom and bath. *Nice, lots of room.* She spied a dresser near a huge window and vowed to check that out at greater length at some point.

Piggy trotted down the stairs; her feet were unaccustomed to hardwood floors. She loved the feel of them and the sound her nails made as they clicked against them. *Hmmm, nice sized rooms. Way bigger than what I was used to.* Piggy peeked into corners and open closets, while she searched for the particular box with the lettering she'd committed to memory. *Hang on, Melvin, I'm coming for you.*

Piggy scooted down one more flight of stairs into the darkened basement below where most of the boxes were strewn about. While her human busied himself in the rooms above, she climbed over piles of items from the old home, and carefully checked every box. She couldn't come up with anything that resembled the box Melvin had crawled into. She slunk around and prodded her paws into crevices and, still, there was no Melvin. Meowing furiously, she called her friend's name again and again, and hoped that she'd hear the scratching of his tiny claws. Still, she heard nothing.

Piggy retraced her steps back up to the rooms above and again to the second floor. She sniffed at every box she came upon; she knew the scent of her pal but could not find it anywhere.

When Matt called Piggy to curl up in bed later that night, she'd been down in the basement for another look. Matt called out again and, reluctantly, Piggy trudged up the stairs to the voice of her human. She jumped onto his bed as he brought her close to his chest, but her mind was elsewhere: riddled with fear for her friend.

Melvin rubbed his small behind from all the jostling that had gone on earlier. It was quiet and darker now than he'd ever remembered. Something didn't feel quite right; it had been hours since he'd heard Matt's friends moving the boxes; hours since anybody had been talking. He didn't remember his box being hoisted out of the truck. Had he been asleep perhaps? Where was Piggy? Surely she'd have been looking for him already?

Melvin scratched against the cardboard. He shoved against DVD cases and scattered them around. *"Help meeee!"* he cried. He heard no sounds around him at all.

Several plush toys sat in the box with Melvin. He couldn't quite make them out, but one felt like a monkey, or an ape. Melvin tugged at the toy and climbed as high as he could to push against the top of the box. The tape was loose and he managed to push and gnaw his way to the outside. He only found more darkness. What on earth?

Melvin scampered down the side of the box. Where was Piggy? Most importantly: where was he? The tiny bit of light coming from a crack several feet away from him confirmed that he was still in the moving van. Nothing else but a few bungee cords, some ratty old blankets, and dust were in there with him. His lone box had been forgotten, stuck in the back of the truck under a covering of some sort.

Panic settled full bloom into Melvin's stomach. Trapped! No food, no friend, and he had no idea where he was. Melvin climbed back into the box resting against the toy monkey and cried himself to sleep.

"She's losing weight," Piggy heard Matt's voice on the phone. "I'm getting concerned. Maybe she's unhappy in the new house."

Piggy reclined in front of the couch. Though her stomach growled, she couldn't eat. It had been three days since she'd seen Melvin. Though she'd tried to find him, there was no box in the house that held him. She'd lost her sister Vision, and now she'd lost her best little pal, too. She slept all hours of the day and night. Being awake depressed her.

Matt placed Piggy into the cat carrier later that day and took her to the v-e-t-s. She didn't care. She'd been responsible for Melvin and hadn't been able to help him make it safely to the new house.

A kindly old veterinarian listened to her heart and lungs, pressed into her belly and peered into her ears. Piggy heard the man say: "She's fine, son. Not a thing wrong with this kitty. As I see it, she's lonely. You said she lost her sister over a year or so ago? Perhaps it's time for a new companion. That may perk her up. Try this new cat kibble out at home too. She'll come around."

Matt left with Piggy, and the worry on his face erased a bit. "Piggy, you gotta start eating again." His cell phone rang just then.

"Hello. Yes, this is Matt. What? Oh wow, thanks." Matt laid the phone onto the seat of his car beside the cat carrier.

"The moving truck company just called. They have another box of mine," he laughed.

Piggy perked up. *Another box? Melvin!*

Matt brought his cat home first and then left to pick up his box. Piggy paced the house over and over; she silently prayed that her friend was in it and safe. She even managed to eat a little of the new kibble but decided it tasted like sawdust.

That night when Matt returned, Piggy couldn't believe her eyes. The writing on the box said: STUFF FOR THE NEW HOUSE. It had to be the one! Lucky for her, Matt put it in the basement to deal with later.

Piggy wasted no time. As she tapped on the side of the box, she whispered, "Melvin, you in there?" She didn't hear a thing. "Mel, can you hear me?" The tiniest scratching came from inside the box. Piggy gnawed at the tape and ripped it away with her claws. The top of the box opened the tiniest bit and Melvin emerged, a bit worse for wear, but in one piece.

"Never again," he said. "That was terrible; all the bouncing and jostling around, and then days without food. Oh! I have such a headache, Piggy." Melvin rubbed at his temples, his tiny fingers hard at work.

Piggy scooped her friend into an embrace that should have crushed him. She bathed his dusty fur while she cried.

"I thought I lost you," she said. "Oh Mel, I'm so glad you're here." She patted his back with her paw. "You must be starving," she said,

"You're skin and bones. I'll be right back with some food for you." Piggy disappeared for a few minutes but returned with small pieces of cat kibble. Melvin ate with gusto and crunched into every precious morsel.

"What happened?" Piggy asked.

"I guess they didn't see my box. It was way back in the truck with some stupid covering over it." Melvin shuddered. "I was so scared, so alone. I thought I'd die."

"Well, you're here now, friend," Piggy said. And if cats could smile, she certainly did so.

"At any rate, we're both here now: home; our new place. Oh, just wait until you see all the room upstairs." Piggy groomed her friend again until he shook himself off, fluffing the fur in all directions."

"Mel, we lost all your old belongings; your beautiful watch is gone."

"I know, Piggy. But we almost lost each other. It's just stuff. I bet I can find some awesome new things in this house."

"Mel, hop on my back. I'm going to show you to your new room."

When all was quiet, Piggy made her way from the basement to show her friend the new kitchen. Melvin climbed counters; he poked into cupboards and shoved bags of chips around until he found an open bag. Zesty Doritos spilled onto the counter and Melvin began to stuff his cheeks with them. Piggy let her friend eat a bit longer, knowing Matt was fast asleep upstairs.

She brought Melvin to the small spare bedroom which housed one single bed, a chest of drawers, a wooden rocking chair, and a deep closet on one end. The room had an L shape to it; around the bend, a small door set into the wall housed the stepladder to the attic. It was easy to pry open, with an improper fit of the door, and it had an inch deep space that Melvin could easily crawl under.

"It's perfect, Piggy," Melvin squealed. "I'm going to love it." He touched his tiny whiskered nose to Piggy's, as they said goodnight to one another.

Exhausted, Piggy nudged Matt's bedroom door open and glanced around. He was asleep in the center of his new queen-sized bed. A computer table and assortment of unopened boxes were strewn about.

Piggy jumped onto the dresser near the window. The screen was open to the cool nighttime air. Her whiskers pressed against it, and she scanned the view below. Never before had she seen such an assortment of rodents, nocturnal creatures, or even deer on the move. *Oh, I'm going to like this.*

About an hour later, she crawled into bed with Matt, and turned herself around and around to find the most comfortable spot. She could hear his steady breathing and he moved a little to accommodate her body; his arm reached out to pull her closer and cuddle with him. Feeling content and loved, Piggy fell asleep instantly and dreamed of adventure, fun, food, and friendship.

Four

Piggy opened her eyes and shivered in the chill of the early winter morning. The wind howled outside and rattled the panes of glass in the windows. She looked over to her human's spot on the bed and saw that he was already gone for the day.

Piggy settled in to make herself presentable: she licked her paw, scrubbed over her face and ears, and nibbled between her toes in the way all cats do, careful to clean every crevice with her hind leg poised in the air. Out of the corner of her eye, she spied Melvin in the hallway sneaking along the baseboard.

"Psst," Piggy called. "Matt's not here, Mel. Come on in." She put her leg down and patted the top of the bed with her paw. Melvin scampered into Matt's bedroom and climbed the quilted comforter with a few small scrambles of his hind legs. Once he was up, he stood on his back feet with his nose pointing in the air, agog with curiosity.

"How did you sleep?" Piggy asked. But Melvin didn't seem to hear her. He jumped around like a mousy cheerleader. "Look, oh, look!" Melvin pointed near Matt's computer where a melted bowl of ice cream sat from the night before. "Good thing your human isn't a neat freak." Melvin flew off the bed in a hurry and beat Piggy to the bowl.

Vanilla ice cream and a smattering of rainbow sprinkles rimmed the bottom of the dish. One lone candy gummy worm sat off to the side. Melvin scooped the candy into his clutches and set off nibbling the wormy headfirst. Piggy lapped up the puddle of ice cream and crunched the sprinkles with her back teeth.

"Melvin, just look at you," Piggy commented. The last of the gummy worm dangled from his mouth. His cheeks were puffed out from stuffing himself full of the candy. He slurped the rest of the body in, and then began licking his paws to remove all traces of stickiness.

"How's your room?" Piggy asked, as she jumped down from the computer desk onto the hardwood floor, amused the sound her nails made when she walked about.

"I'm pretty much done with all the decorating. I'd love for you to see it later. If you can squeeze through the door, that is," Melvin whispered as an afterthought.

"I heard that," Piggy said. "Thanks for insulting me." She walked away from her pal, tail indignantly in the air. "Humph!"

Piggy ran down the stairs to the first floor, Melvin close behind. "Sorry Piggy, I didn't mean anything by it."

"No, of course you didn't," Piggy said, as she rolled her eyes and tried to keep a distance between her and Melvin. She jumped onto the back of the couch to sharpen her claws into the cushion. A bit of fluff poked from a small hole she'd made, and she batted at it for a while. She pulled harder and out popped a wad. Piggy tried stuffing it back into the hole but then gave up to swat it behind the couch.

Next, she busied herself with a soft afghan thrown over the arm of the sofa. Using the delicate pads of her paws, she kneaded the blanket over and over, the scent of her human embedded in it.

All the while, Melvin ran about trying to get Piggy's attention. "Piggy, I said I was sorry." Nothing. She ignored him as if he wasn't there. Melvin slunk away, wiry brown tail between his legs, head hung low as he trudged back up to the second floor.

Humph. Serves him right, Piggy thought. I'm tired of the snide remarks about my weight. I'll show him a thing or two. I won't speak to him for a few days. Then when he misses me, he'll come crawling back, begging me for forgiveness.

Piggy curled around on the fuzzy blanket laying her head into her paws; her whipcord tail curled around herself and fell into blissful slumber.

Much later, Piggy woke to notice how dim it was in the room, almost as if the light had been sucked right out of the day. Fat, lazy snowflakes began to fall. Feathery and lacey, they cascaded through the air to light on bushes and grass. Piggy jumped from the couch onto the windowsill; her breath made a frosty fog on the glass. *Brrr, it's really cold in here now.*

She thought about the Christmas holiday, only a few short weeks away. It is always one of her favorite times of the year. In the past she'd always enjoyed watching Matt and his uncle decorate and pile colorful, wrapped presents under the tree. Most of all, Piggy liked guessing which ones were for her.

Matt had a small artificial Christmas tree in the corner of their new living room. Colorful twinkle lights covered every branch and home-made ornaments from his youth hung from tiny hooks. When Matt wasn't looking, Piggy pawed at the fake bark of the tree and played with the hanging decorations.

She couldn't wait for the silly cartoons Matt watched year after year: The Grinch, Frosty, and Rudolph. She loved the festive music her human played day and night. Nothing was better though, than all the foods that would soon come through their door. Matt's mom and grandma made the most wonderful treats during the holiday. Christmas

Eve was best since they prepared several types of fish. Piggy's mouth watered just thinking about it all.

She loved the attention and warmth as Matt's family gathered together. *Humans are very fortunate to have such a wonderful time of the year.*

The snow fell harder outside blanketing every surface as Piggy continued watching and daydreaming. The wind raged and blew the sparkling diamonds of white all around. A huge burst of wind gusted and the front door to the house flew open.

What on earth? Piggy crouched down with her ears flattened to her head and a ball of fear in her stomach. She'd never seen such a thing happen before. *Didn't Matt lock up behind himself this morning?*

Tufts of snow swirled into the house and the wind pushed with great force. A tiny bell on the Christmas tree tinkled as the wind blew past Piggy. She sat immobilized, terrified at what she was seeing.

Just as suddenly as the wind had picked up, it stopped. Snow covered the hardwood floor of the living room in crunchy piles. Piggy, a bit wary, though curious, hopped down from her perch to investigate.

"Hello Piggy." She stopped cold in her tracks, a most familiar voice calling her name. "Piggy, it's me. Look."

Where the door stood open and the snow covered the floor, a velvet gray cat sat and stared at her. Piggy blinked once, twice, trying to clear her sight. The cat smiled, her large golden eyes alight with humor. A soft glow emanated from around her.

"How are you dear sister?" The voice was music to Piggy's ears; the lovely, familiar voice of a sister who had been with her through thick and thin, good times and bad. *It can't be.*

"Vision? My goodness! How can this be?

You're uh, you're. . ." Piggy shook herself.

"May I come in?" the gray cat asked as if it was the most normal question in the world. She didn't wait for Piggy to answer and padded through the carpet of snow before her. Vision stopped right in front of Piggy and touched her with a delicate paw.

"Oh Piggy, it's grand to see you!" Vision rubbed herself against her sister, purring.

Piggy began crying then and laid a paw over her back. The soft feel of her velvet coat was such a welcome touch. Her heart fluttered in her chest, and she felt a way that she would never be able to describe. The sniffling slowed, and the cats smiled, both joyful to be in each other's company.

"I have so much to tell you," Vision said. "I only have a short time, though." She looked around the room. "This is a lovely home. I'm happy for you and Matt."

The cats jumped onto the couch, and Piggy forgot the fact the front door stood wide open; it wasn't cold in the room though.

"How has your life been, sister dear?" Vision asked.

Piggy spoke then about her newer friends, Melvin, Rolf, and all the creatures that had helped rescue her pal during such a dark time.

"I'm so pleased," Vision said. Her soft voice held a touch of higher speech, almost as if she'd gone to school and learned to speak more distinctly.

Piggy would think later that her sister seemed almost regal. She carried herself with a different air than when she'd known her and loved her in all the years they'd been together.

Vision laid a paw over her sister. "I want you to know there's so much more than what your eyes see, Piggy. There's a whole new world, the rainbow bridge and beyond. I thought that you should know." She sighed, a sad smile on her pretty face, her white whiskers almost shone.

"This time of the year, Christmas, is very special. Treat it special. Treat those you love with respect and kindness. It all comes back to you."

"Vision, have I done something wrong?" Piggy asked as she pulled away from her sister.

"Oh no, Piggy, no; this is my gift to you. This is the magic of the Christmas season. I chose to spend it with you whom I loved more than any other creature."

Vision licked her paw and washed it over Piggy's head just as she'd done so many times before. Piggy basked in her radiance and warmth. The feel of her sister's touch comforted her.

"Can you stay?" Piggy whispered. "Please, I don't want to lose you again."

"I'm never far away," Vision said. "Don't worry about anything and remember to live every day to the fullest. Have fun and laugh often. And by all means, be open to different things. Life changes so easily and sometimes if we open ourselves to something new, it may be for the best."

Vision hopped down from the couch. The day had grown still while she'd been speaking and now the wind had picked up once again. A blustery gust blew in and the bell on the Christmas tree tinkled once more; just like that, Vision was gone.

Piggy closed her eyes and hoped when she opened them, her sister would be there before her again. This time there was nothing. The front door was closed as if it had never blown open. The snow stopped falling and Piggy heard the sound of a car door just then. *Surely, I've been dreaming...*

A few minutes later, Matt walked through the door, bags upon bags in his arms. "Wait until you see what you're getting for Christmas, Piggy," he said, placing his purchases on the loveseat near the door. "No peeking."

Piggy, at a loss for meows, couldn't break the spell she felt at seeing her sister. Speechless, Piggy sat to stare off into the distance, and did not hear a word that her human said.

"What's the matter?" Matt asked, as he walked over to her and patted her head. "You're awfully quiet." Piggy managed a small, soft purr to appease Matt, but scampered from the couch and headed up the stairs to see Melvin. Her actions from earlier nagged at her and she was eager to see her friend.

Piggy slipped into the guest bedroom and headed to the attic door. She pawed at it several times, scratching with her nails. Melvin's small head peeked out a minute later and his face burst into the biggest smile.

"Piggy, I'm so glad you're here. I'm so sorry for this morning. I should never have said that to you."

"No, Mel, I'm the one who's sorry. I treated you rudely. Forgive me?"

Melvin hugged Piggy as the two heard Matt's footfalls on the stairs. "I'll be back later, Mel." She met her human in the hallway.

"What are you doing, Piggy?" Matt asked, as he bent down and scooped her into his arms. "You're acting weird."

Well, Matt, let's see. I just saw a ghost and maybe, just maybe that's what's eating at me.

Piggy began to purr and snuggled under her human's chin. Matt carried her into his room and set her on the bed in her favorite spot. Worn out from her adventure, she fell fast asleep.

The weeks flew by and finally Christmas Eve arrived. Piggy helped Melvin decorate his huge room in the attic, by sneaking bits of tinsel and tiny ornaments to him from time to time. He had a small pipe cleaner Christmas tree propped in the far corner. A plastic reindeer with glittery horns stood nearby.

Melvin stored his stash of treats in an old Tupperware container. His bed was a shoebox with a few pieces of old blanket pulled from the basement tucked into a cozy section of the room.

"Mel, I can't believe the size of this room. At our old house you had a small hole in the wall. Now you have the whole top of the house to yourself."

"Ho, ho, ho," Melvin chuckled, and he pulled a bit of cotton fluff from an old box of Q-Tips. He put the cotton under his chin, a miniscule Santa resplendent in a small red sweater he'd swiped from one of Matt's stuffed animals. Piggy sat back on her haunches and laughed until tears came from her eyes.

The two friends exchanged gifts. Piggy gave Melvin several pieces of Swiss cheese which had fallen earlier from the counter in the kitchen. Melvin handed her the most adorable ball of fuzzy red yarn he'd snatched from another old box in the basement. They talked late into the night as the snow fell harder outside the small attic window.

Several times Piggy thought of telling Melvin about the ghostly visit from her sister. She didn't think he'd believe her. Piggy didn't know what to believe either. Yet she'd felt a calmness since that day, a feeling there was so much more than what her eyes could see. She decided to keep the story to herself.

Matt's family arrived at noon: Gram Eileen, Pap Rich, whom he affectionately called Lamp, Matt's sweet little mom, Karen, and his Uncle Rick. Gram and Pap were up in age, a cute twosome who bickered a bit, but secretly adored one another.

Each family member petted Piggy and fussed over her as they rested mountains of colorful gifts beneath Matt's tree. Piggy pawed at one particular package until Matt shooed her away.

The next few hours, Matt's mom and grandma tore through cabinets, whisked items into bowls, and opened and closed the oven door several times. Wonderful smells floated through the air to Piggy's delicate nose. She sat on a fuzzy rug in the dining room away from all the commotion.

Uncle Rick and Lamp played video games in the living room. Piggy heard the sound of Sega pinball and trotted into the room to investigate. She jumped near the television screen and batted at the ball as it floated around.

At four o'clock in the afternoon, Gram Eileen announced dinner was ready. The family gathered around the dining room table to hold hands and be thankful for many blessings. Bowls and platters traveled around the table, and Piggy knew this was her cue. She snuck under the table to position herself under the tangle of legs and shoes and wait for the precious morsels to fall.

Ah, my first victim. A piece of haddock tumbled off the edge of the table and Piggy snatched it up before any of the humans could notice. She licked her chops, and the wonderful taste of fish flooded her mouth. A few other crumbs fell near her, but Piggy seemed most delighted when Matt's mom placed a small dish on the kitchen floor with a few tender pieces of fish for her. Piggy rubbed Karen's ankles in appreciation and gave her the best Cheshire cat smile; it had won her compliments in the past.

It took a while for the women to clean the table and dishes after dinner. The men basked in the warmth of the living room and rearranged presents by name. Piggy stole over to her own small pile and tapped the curly red ribbon with her paw. She thought it was a bit odd there were so few gifts for her. Finally, the ladies were through with their work. They came into the living room, while Matt passed out gifts to everyone.

The family is no stranger to lengthy gift opening. It took almost two hours for everyone to unwrap their treasures. Piggy received a bag of furry mice, a tinkle bell toy, and burlap bag of catnip. She rubbed on everyone's legs as the family laughed into the night and told stories from past holidays.

One by one, the family members made their way out later. Matt stood at the window with Piggy in his arms and waved goodbye. "Remember Piggy, you didn't get your big gift yet. I'm not sure when it's arriving." He placed her onto the floor and patted her head. "Merry Christmas."

On Christmas morning, Piggy awoke to another beautiful snowfall. Several inches had arrived through the night; the ground was a blanket of white. Matt put on a ski coat and gloves and headed out to shovel the driveway. Piggy watched from her perch on the living room window for a bit, and then headed over to the Christmas tree standing on hind legs to reach up for a new ornament that Matt had received as a gift. The "First Year in a New House" had a young man and his cat standing in front of their home. Piggy pawed at it and made it rock back and forth on the branch.

"Quit it, Piggy," Matt yelled behind her. She stopped what she was doing and turned to her owner. His cheeks were red with the cold, and he shivered as he peeled layers of clothing from his body.

"I'm going to Gram's today," Matt said. "You behave and tonight we'll play together. I hope you liked your little presents." He ran partway up the stairs and turned back to her. "The big surprise is coming sometime next week." His eyes twinkled with mischief, and then he disappeared to get ready for the day.

Melvin and I will have hours to ourselves today.

Around noon, Melvin and Piggy busied themselves riffling through the kitchen. A plate of sugar cookies from Matt's mother sat wrapped on top of the counter. A basket filled with cheddar snack crackers lie uncovered nearby. Melvin scurried up the dishtowel that hung from the oven door while Piggy hopped up behind him. She lifted the corner of the cling wrap that covered the cookies while Melvin snatched two of them. The two friends crunched cheesy crackers afterward until they thought they'd burst.

PIGGY THE CAT AND ARCADE MATT

With full bellies, they settled in for a nap at the foot of the Christmas tree. Melvin fit perfectly into the stable of the manger set. Piggy was content to lay by his side.

After they woke up a bit later, Melvin had one of his adventurous ideas: Matt had received a toy train set to place around the base of the tree as one of his gifts. His grandfather helped him set it up the night before. It frightened Piggy as she watched it whizz and clack around the track. It tooted its whistle each time it made a pass. Now Melvin wanted a ride, and he wanted Piggy to operate it. They walked around several times to locate the start and stop buttons and make sure that the track was snapped together well.

"Piggy, I'm going to climb into the caboose at the back of the train. It's perfectly mouse-sized. Ooh, this is going to be such fun," Melvin clapped his paws with glee.

Piggy, the cautious, asked: "Mel, are you sure you'll be okay? This thing went pretty fast last night. I don't want you to hurt yourself."

"Nonsense," Melvin said. "You're such a worry wart. I'm going to pretend I'm on a trip to a faraway land. Come on, start it up." Melvin climbed into the train; his paws perched on the sides and his long tail stuck out from behind. His eyes gleamed with excitement.

Well, okay then...

Piggy pawed the start button and away the train chugged. Round and round it went while Melvin yelled "whoopee!" Each time he passed Piggy, he'd let her know how much closer he was to his imaginary destination. When he'd finally had enough, Piggy stopped the train with the click of a paw.

"That was great! Oh Piggy, I wish you could have come along."

"I'm fine with four feet on the ground," she said. "Come on Mel, let's get you out of there." Piggy put a paw out to help her friend from the caboose. As Melvin began to hop from the cab, he realized his tail was stuck in part of the track.

"Hee, hee," he laughed a bit nervously. "It seems like my tail's caught." He pulled at it and nothing happened.

"Come on, Melvin, this isn't funny," Piggy said. "Stop acting like you can't get it out. That's enough of your adventures for one day."

"No, I'm not playing, Piggy. My tail's wedged in this piece of track. Help me, please." Melvin's voice grew panicked.

Piggy crouched closer and tried to gently wiggle Melvin's tail from the part of track it was stuck under. Nothing happened. Melvin tugged and squealed.

"Ouch, Piggy, it hurts. What are we going to do?"

Piggy glanced at the clock on the wall; it was four in the afternoon. Matt shouldn't be home for a few hours, she hoped. She jumped past Melvin to the other side of the track near the manger set and knocked the plaster figurines askew. She extended her paw and tried to pry the tail from the new angle. She had no success.

"Uh, Melvin, I'm not sure what we're going to do. I can't budge anything."

Melvin began to cry. "I'm done for Piggy. That's all. Your human is going to come home and find a mouse stuck in his train set. Then it's all over."

Melvin has a point. Matt won't just walk through the door and say, oh, there's a cute little mouse caught in my new train set. Let me let him go. No, it probably won't end well.

Piggy flattened herself to the ground and tried again. Melvin shivered and whimpered, and she had to stop several times to calm him down. The clock ticked on to five p.m.

"Mel, I can't even see where your tail is caught." Piggy hunched further and squinted.

PIGGY THE CAT AND ARCADE MATT

"Wait a minute," she said. "I can at least remove the portion of track your tail is wedged into. This way you can at least get away until we think of another brilliant plan."

"I'm doomed! Doomed, Piggy. That will never work." Theatrical Melvin put a paw to his forehead to resemble the world's smallest hero about to say goodbye to the world.

"Stop it, silly," Piggy said. She worked at the portion of track his tail disappeared into. At last, the piece slipped free.

They ran up the stairs, Melvin with the piece of train track still stuck to his tail; it clattered and clinked the whole way. They ran into the spare bedroom to sit and think.

"As I see it," Piggy said, examining the situation, "we either have to wedge the plastic apart since you're stuck in the middle slat, or find some way to slide that tail out of there without breaking the thing."

Another hour ticked by. "I've got it." Piggy nudged her friend from behind. "Let's head to the kitchen. There's a bottle of olive oil on the counter. Oil's slippery, you see. If we can get some around the tail and piece of track, it may just pop right out."

"Oh brother," Melvin said. "You're gonna coat me with that stuff? *Ewww...* I don't like it one bit."

"You got a better plan then?"

"Well, uh, no."

"Then come on, we don't have much time." Piggy raced back down the stairs, and Melvin clacked along behind her. *Step clack, step clack.* At last, he reached the kitchen where Piggy had already jumped onto the counter.

"Mel, I'm going to have to get this bottle to the floor somehow so you can unscrew the cap. Thank goodness it's plastic, so it won't break. Watch out below!" Piggy nudged the small bottle closer to the counter's edge. Little by little she pushed at it, and at last, it fell to the kitchen tile with a plop.

Melvin stared up at his friend, still doubtful, but began to work at the cap with his little claws and hands.

"I'm too tired, Piggy, it's too hard."

Piggy jumped onto the floor beside her friend. "You can do it, Mel. Come on, we don't have much time."

After a few more tries, the cap was free. Olive oil spilled onto the floor. Piggy wasted no time as she slathered it onto her paw and coated the piece of track's front and back. She dipped her friend's tail into the puddle until it looked like an oily brown worm.

"Oh the shame, the horrible embarrassment of this," Melvin prattled as his friend pawed at the stuck tail. Little by little, Piggy worked it free. The two of them were so involved in their dilemma they hadn't heard the front door open or Matt enter the house.

The kitchen light clicked on. Piggy and Melvin froze.

"What's this?" Matt screamed, reaching for the mouse with a gloved hand. But as he walked another step, his feet fell from under him, and he slipped in the olive oil toppling to the floor.

Piggy grabbed Melvin in her mouth and ran from the room as fast as her little legs would carry her, right up the stairs into the spare room and directly to the attic door.

"Here, Mel, disappear. I'll have to go back down to Matt and see what happened."

When Piggy returned to the kitchen, she found Matt on his feet, mopping up the mess. In one hand, he held the piece of train track with a most puzzled look on his face.

"Piggy, I have no idea what just happened, but I'm really proud of you. You got that old mouse. Great job." Matt set the piece of track upon the counter. "You listen to me, though," he continued. "No more jumping on counters, okay?" He waggled a finger at her.

"You shouldn't be playing with my stuff," Matt said and indicated the oily piece of train track in his hands. "Oh well, after tomorrow, I won't have to worry about this anymore." He finished mopping up the floor and rubbed his behind where he'd fallen and hurt himself.

Piggy gulped. After tomorrow; what did that mean? Was her human planning on getting rid of her? She slunk from the kitchen and headed straight to the attic.

"Oh Piggy, he can't be serious." Melvin finished licking his fur; the oil taste made him shudder. His brown coat gleamed.

"Then why did Matt say that?" Piggy asked her friend. "I'm afraid he's had it with me, Mel. This was probably the last straw." She sprawled out on the floor next to the mouse and put her head in her paws, a sigh escaping.

Melvin scuttled over to her. "We can think of something. Maybe we can get you out of this house somehow. You can hide outside. He'll never find you."

But Piggy wasn't comforted. She later heard Matt calling for her, but she never left the attic room that night. If he truly was fed up with her and the antics she had pulled, she may as well spend her last night with her best buddy.

Sleep didn't come easy, and Piggy tossed and turned. Nightmares plagued her: scary scenes of animal shelters and large barking dogs with huge fangs. She woke up the next morning with a sinking feeling in the pit of her stomach.

"Where were you, silly cat?" Matt asked as he poured Piggy's favorite Purina crunchies into her bowl. "Didn't you hear me calling?"

What's the use? Piggy thought. *You don't love me anymore.*

She could barely choke down a few pieces of cat kibble. It was odd because Matt seemed in high spirits; he whistled while he popped his frozen waffles into the toaster.

"Piggy, this is your special day. Remember I told you I had a huge surprise for you? Well, later you'll get to see what it is. I'm headed out for a few hours, but I'll be back with it later." Matt patted her head while Piggy stared up at him with a most blank expression on her face.

Well, well, she thought, *Not only am I staying, but I'm getting a present!* Phew, that was close. Piggy ran to her food bowl and wolfed down a large quantity of cat chow.

A little later in the morning, Piggy sat in Matt's bedroom window looking at the snow-covered trees and the neighbors' houses. She heard the front door open, and Matt's voice call out.

"Piggy, come here. Wait 'til you see."

Just then, her sister's words came back to her. The ones she'd said at the end of their Christmas visit: *"Be open to new things."* She couldn't understand why she'd thought of them right then, but the words resonated loudly, as almost a promise.

Piggy tiptoed down the stairs while Matt set a cardboard box onto the floor of the living room. A strange scratching sound came from within. What on earth?

"Well, Piggy," Matt said while he opened the top of the box. "I know you've been lonely since Vision left us. I wanted to get you a friend. Someone you can take care of." He placed his hands into the box and scooped out a tiny grey-striped kitten. Piggy took a step back to hiss at the squirming ball of fur in his hands.

This is it? The big surprise? Thanks a lot, Matt. I think I'd rather not.

The kitten hopped down and scrambled over to Piggy. She rubbed herself against Piggy's legs and began to purr; her big green eyes lit with wonder and innocence.

Matt stood back watching them with a genuine smile on his face.

Okay, Piggy thought. *I'll play along for his sake.* She let the kitten bat at her tail but swatted her a few times when she became too playful and rough. "This is Goober," Matt said. "It means 'little peanut'. That's just what she is." He crouched on the floor with his cats and set some new furry toy mice and jingle balls near them.

Maybe Matt's right. Maybe another cat will be a welcome addition to our home. We both missed Vision so much and Goober will surely fill the void. Now there would be the three of us.

Piggy allowed the kitten to sidle up next to her.

Oh no! Wait! What about Melvin? Piggy groaned as she thought about what this could mean: Goober must be taught that a mouse could be a friend. It would take time, patience, and lots of restraint.

Well, I'm up to the task, Piggy thought. *This means so much to Matt, and besides, what else do I have to do right now?* Lifting her face upward, Piggy winked at her sister, Vision. She could do this. She could do anything.

The End

About the Author

With a vivid imagination, the lessons learned in childhood, and the love of a close, Italian family, Karen began writing heartfelt, inspirational fiction novels, one which closely follows many of the conversations she and her mother shared through the years: *Reflections From my Mother's Kitchen: A Journey of Healing and Hope.*

When her mother began showing signs of Alzheimer's- type- dementia in the last several years, Karen once again stepped into the role of caregiver for her aging parents along with the help of a wonderful brother. It was watching the love between her parents into the golden years which inspired her fiction novels about dementia: *Love Woven in Time,* and *Love Finds a Way.*

Karen has been active mentoring young writers, speaking at local libraries, schools, and care facilities. Recently she became a member of AlzAuthors, a loving community of writers dedicated to encouraging caregivers and family members of loved ones with dementia and Alzheimer's. Karen is a passionate advocate for the elderly. Her walk with God has given her the inspiration to blog about losing her parents and their family's journey from grief to healing and other heartfelt, encouraging tales.

Several of Karen's stories were recently chosen by Guidepost's sister magazines for publication. "The Earrings" appeared in *Mysterious Ways* magazine, "The Memory Blanket," in *Angels on Earth, and* "Merry Christmas Mom and Dad," as well as a few others.

More recently, she wrote a loving memoir about her parents, "Bushel and a Peck: Hope, Healing and Unconditional Love," which has been well-received in the Alzheimer's and mental health communities.

She lives in Pennsylvania with her husband Jim and their two furry cats, Rocco and Bella.

You can follow Karen on her blog:

http://karenmalena.blogspot.com/

Other socials:

https://www.amazon.com/stores/Karen-Malena/author/B005TH0F0Y?ref=ap_rdr&store_ref=ap_rdr&isDramIntegrated=true&shoppingPortalEnabled=true

https://www.facebook.com/profile.php?id=100063483639851

https://www.goodreads.com/author/show/5260052.Karen_Malena

https://www.instagram.com/karenlmalena/

https://twitter.com/arcade_mom

https://www.pinterest.com/karenmalena/

Made in the USA
Middletown, DE
21 April 2024

53270421R00073